Lincoln, Leadership and Gettysburg

Defining Moments of Greatness

Glen Aubrey

Creative Team Publishing

Creative Team Publishing
San Diego

First Printing

ISBN: 978-0-9797358-8-2
PUBLISHED BY CREATIVE TEAM PUBLISHING
www.CreativeTeamPublishing.com
San Diego

Printed in the United States of America

Lincoln, Leadership and Gettysburg

Defining Moments of Greatness

Glen Aubrey

Effects endure beyond the events that give them life.

Learn their truths.

History's lessons shape the minds and means of generations.

Table of Contents

Prologue

"If we could first know where we are, and whither we are tending, we could better judge what to do, and how to do it."

This sentence is the opening line of Abraham Lincoln's "A House Divided" speech, delivered before the Republican State Convention of Illinois at Springfield on June 17, 1858.

These words display several strong characteristics of the man and his leadership: his penchant toward logical reasoning, commitment to base decisions on carefully weighed information, and thoughtful deliberation to get to a topic's central idea.

Many speeches were to follow this one, of course, and many had preceded it. Throughout those that history has marked as monumental and worthy of remembrance, we discover threads of greatness woven through enduring principle. The challenge is to learn why the principles he articulated have endured and how to apply them, because they still live. Further, if we want to add value to experience and legacy to life, we will lead others to do likewise.

In Lincoln's public proclamations, before and during his presidency, he thought long and hard before he spoke. We know he expressed discomfort with any lack of preparation.

Then, as today, words from a president were taken seriously. Words of a figure so public, especially words spoken lightly or thoughtlessly, could cause severe misunderstanding, breed confusion, produce momentous upheaval, or worse. Words whose time and timing were right, however, could promote best actions and problem resolution. Thoughtfully rehearsed subject matter, carefully articulated and founded upon unshakable truth, could achieve great results.

Reflect on his content and context, motives and methods, platform and perspective, and to whom his speeches were presented. Considerations like these were communication hallmarks of Lincoln. He weighed words and their meanings very carefully before uttering them—and this in a day when the president wrote his own speeches.

Lincoln, Leadership and Gettysburg is a book that describes profound leadership principles evidenced in the words of what many believe is one of Lincoln's greatest orations, the Gettysburg Address. This two minute speech was delivered at Gettysburg, Pennsylvania on November 19, 1863, as part of the dedication ceremonies of a national cemetery. This event occurred a mere four months following the conclusion of the Gettysburg Campaign, where General Robert E. Lee's Army of Northern Virginia had been engaged in a fierce three-day invasive battle against General George Gordon Meade's Army of the Potomac. Meade himself had just been promoted to the assignment of army commander on June 28, 1863, only three days prior to the opening shots. The battle had resulted in some 50,000 casualties over July 1, 2, and 3. The small town would take years to recover. Its legacy would be changed forever.

Visiting Gettysburg today, viewing the vicinity where the ceremony occurred, guests are struck with the solemnity of the place. The area hosts mature and majestic trees, expansive vistas, manicured grassy slopes, small American flags marking graves, enduring stone and marble monuments, silent cannons and, for those who ponder the sacrifice of the men who fought there, a hush of the sacred.

Travel there. Do as many leaders have done and more should do. Pause a long moment to reflect upon the supreme causes for which soldiers fought. Remain quiet and thankful in your contemplation. Breathe deeply the living air of soulful appreciation. Our freedom was purchased by men and women who, like the combatants donning blue or gray, offered all they could give on behalf of those who would live after them.

As the nation's war-time leader, Lincoln was invited to deliver "a few appropriate remarks" as part of the dedication ceremony. Following a two-hour oration by Edward Everett, the most highly acclaimed orator of the day, Lincoln was introduced by his friend, Ward Hill Lamon, and began his remarks.

It is curious to note that there are no photographs of President Lincoln speaking—the speech was concluded before the cameraman had enough time to prepare and take his shot. Photographs of the procession and assembled crowds were taken both in the town and at the cemetery. One even captured Lincoln seated, but a record on film of the actual speaking event was not made. Only through the written record do we know of his mortal words that enveloped immortal truths.

Audio recording was decades to come, of course. Contemporary accounts noted that Lincoln's voice was high and piercing.

Have you ever wondered what his voice really sounded like? What ambient noises competed for the crowd's attention? How restless were the people after standing for 120 minutes to hear Everett? What were Lincoln's facial expressions, gestures, appeal, and stance? For the student of Gettysburg, these are fairly common thoughts—and we can only wonder at the answers.

After the event, Mr. Everett wrote a note to Lincoln: "I should be glad, if I could flatter myself that I came as near to the central idea of the occasion, in two hours, as you did in two minutes."

We do not know for sure whether Lincoln realized at the time that his speech would endure; in a letter to Everett the following day, Lincoln wrote, *"Your kind note of to-day is received. In our respective parts yesterday, you could not have been excused to make a short address, nor I a long one. I am pleased to know that, in your judgment, the little I did say was not entirely a failure."* Perhaps as time went on he felt his words would last after all. We do know Lincoln wrote out a total of at least three different copies of the speech in addition to two preliminary drafts.

The battle of Gettysburg and the Gettysburg Address should be viewed as defining moments of greatness for President Abraham Lincoln, his leadership, and the Union he sought to preserve. Because it is true that Gettysburg, the place, the battle, and the address have played such important roles in our history, we should explore what composes this impressive juxtaposition of incidents and ideas.

What causes words to inspire beyond their utterance in the past, present, and future? What about these remarkable sentences requires profound reflection? Themes within the speech moved those who heard it. Succeeding generations have been greatly impacted as they have pondered the depth and breadth of its contents.

These immortal lines speak volumes to those who desire to learn from Lincoln and live in freedom. Understand why this speech yet breathes long after it was composed and presented and one is better prepared to enjoy and preserve the free country that is the United States of America.

If we choose to position ourselves as students of monumental occurrences and their root causes, there are great truths we can embrace. Much like the opening lines of "A House Divided," we should know where we have been, what brought us to this point, and where on the basis of truth and judgment we should go.

An understanding of history's lessons helps us observe and practice balanced views based on enduring principles. Those who refuse to pay attention to history's repeatable proofs or neglect to apply them will have to learn the same lessons in alternate ways, perhaps at undue costs.

Lincoln's leadership and the Gettysburg Address compose inter-related partnerships of living and lasting values. Principles of law, war, peace, honor, sacrifice, steadfast determination, firm resolve, and true greatness are just a few.

The platforms in the speech build upon foundations that structure standards of purposed endeavor and unshakable endurance. We should learn from Lincoln and use these standards intentionally. These fundamentals contribute to the wellbeing of our human family. They create lasting legacies. We use the standards wisely when we define, declare, and decide what to do on the basis of what is right.

In the Gettysburg Address, the leader of the war-torn nation spoke from history as he positioned the present in order to preserve the Union. A major facet of leadership emerges here: great leadership frames defining moments as it seeks to explain cause and effect. One of the reasons the address still lives is that it continues to inspire others to lead as Lincoln did, regardless of circumstances. Growing leaders learn and earn the responsibilities inherent in preserving and defending great causes.

Lincoln, Leadership and Gettysburg is written for students of principle who want to discover the examples of leadership to be found within the Gettysburg Address. This book is an offering from one who continues to reflect, return to, and learn from these inspirational words and the events surrounding them.

You are invited to join me as an honored guest. We will consider the content and context of the speech. We will grow through this process. What we learn we can then teach to those who follow or lead us.

Address Delivered at the Dedication of the Cemetery at Gettysburg

Fourscore and seven years ago our fathers brought forth on this continent, a new nation, conceived in Liberty, and dedicated to the proposition that all men are created equal.

Now we are engaged in a great civil war, testing whether that nation, or any nation so conceived and so dedicated, can long endure. We are met on a great battlefield of that war. We have come to dedicate a portion of that field, as a final resting place for those who here gave their lives that that nation might live. It is altogether fitting and proper that we should do this.

But, in a larger sense, we cannot dedicate—we cannot consecrate—we cannot hallow—this ground. The brave men, living and dead, who struggled here, have consecrated it, far above our poor power to add or detract. The world will little note, nor long remember what we say here, but it can never forget what they did here. It is for us the living, rather, to be dedicated here to the unfinished work which they who fought here have thus far so nobly advanced. It is rather for us to be here dedicated to the great task remaining before us—that from these honored dead we take increased devotion to that cause for which they gave the last full measure of devotion—that we here highly resolve that these dead shall not have died in vain—that this nation, under God, shall have a new birth of freedom—and that government of the people, by the people, for the people, shall not perish from the earth.

Abraham Lincoln.

November 19, 1863.

Leadership Lessons in the Speech

Essential truths and principles of leadership are presented throughout this book. Several of them are set apart here for the reader's perusal.

Learning becomes living when behaviors change. As you come across these truths you are invited to consider: What principles should I embrace? What behaviors would I be willing to change for me to become a better leader?

- Leaders reflect upon and uphold the supreme causes for which soldiers fight.

- Our freedom was purchased by men and women who, like the soldiers donning blue or gray, offered all they could give on behalf of those who would live after them.

- Great leadership frames defining moments as it seeks to explain cause and effect.

- Growing leaders learn and earn the responsibilities inherent in preserving and defending great causes.

- Learning becomes living when behaviors change.

- History shapes us.

- Leaders who communicate effectively identify with their audience.

- Leaders set frameworks of understanding into which followers position themselves.

- Effective leaders help their followers frame choices against revealed and lasting truth.

- Leaders don't change history—they learn from it. Then they teach the lessons of history to those who follow.

- When one gives his or her life for the benefit of another, that gift represents a payment of immense value in exchange for additional untold values on behalf of those who receive.

- A leader's view of history recognizes, considers, and profoundly appreciates the contributions of those who pay it forward on behalf of others.

- What is cherished today is often composed of what was given up yesterday.

- Leaders observe and weigh history carefully. Life truths emerge from the lessons history teaches for those who appreciate and apply what they learn.

- All human beings possess identical God-given attributes. One is the equality of every individual.

- Leadership's legacies last beyond what is expedient. They rest upon enduring principle, not endless opinion.

- No division, regardless of the degrees of disagreement that may pervade its history, would ever serve to sever the unity of the nation.

- Leaders work for endurance over the long haul.

- The wise leader recognizes that conflicts will be fought; the effective leader chooses where problems should be dealt with.

- History teaches contemporary and future generations the awesome responsibilities that accompany acts of remembering.

- Truths worthy of belief and sacrifice are rehearsed and applied despite pain and adverse circumstances.

- Core principles and practices affect all they touch in every era and location.

- Leaders recognize their limits. How they handle what they don't know is as important as how they handle what they do know.

- Lasting legacies are born and flourish when right communication, core principles, and concrete action cooperate.

- Viewpoints of one generation teach lessons from the past, apply principles in the present, and plan for times yet to come.

- Every action bears a reaction; each cause births an effect.

- Leaders who build legacy recognize their limits and honor the greatness that has preceded them. They consecrate the payments of one generation as they provide a context for current contributions.

- Teachers and leaders who generate living legacies create opportunities for successors to take their places and accomplish more.

- True investors provide benefits they will never enjoy to individuals they will never know.

- The admirable works of one generation are finished well when their leaders prepare those who follow to succeed at greater levels than the current generation.

- The goal for dedicated leaders and followers, devoted teachers and students, is never just to finish. The goal is to finish well.

- Examples of purposeful dedication today become the permanent history lessons of tomorrow.

- People act out of desire when they are convinced of the truth of the leader's words, his or her character, and the viability of the cause the leader represents.

- Leaders notice and praise the people who serve on behalf of a greater cause while recognizing and rewarding their deeds. They openly appreciate the persons *and* their contributions.

- Increased devotion initiates cooperation from people who agree on the merits of an endeavor. When they agree they contribute whatever it takes to make a goal come true.

- When a dream is worth a person's hope and desire, belief in its fulfillment generates action toward achievement. The dedication to make the dream come true is where resilience and perseverance dwell.

- Leadership submits when it recognizes that needs for improvements exist. Leadership perseveres when it determines a course of action is right.

- Effective leaders understand that service *to* their people comes before requiring service *from* their people.

- Exemplary leadership chooses humility before God and dedication to a cause proven to be of greater importance than self absorption or exaggerated promotion.

- All people everywhere should be free.

- When a wise leader recognizes the need for a new birth of freedom that leader chooses humility. When positive changes are desired, that leader submits to higher authority. He or she makes choices based on abiding principles. The leader acts on those principles with determination. Results outlast persons, circumstances, and the opinions of any era.

- Those who are elected represent their constituencies best when they serve the people who placed them in office.

- A principle embraced must be followed by the duty required to uphold it.

- A leader firmly remains not dissuaded from right causes no matter the degrees of difficulty. When the decision to uphold a true principle is declared, a great leader shall not be deterred.

- Dedicated leaders honor and uphold the highest goals for the greatest good.

- Leaders who understand their purpose, place, and responsibility recognize that consequences are not optional. Results always follow actions, good or bad. These leaders prepare for consequences as well as try to fashion them.

- Effects endure beyond the events that give them life.

- What one generation gives in sacrifice, future generations receive in liberty.

- Great leaders stand for the right and serve well the people who elect them when they lead them with integrity, honoring the people's desire and trust.

- It is we who provide the guarantee of perpetuity.

- Conclusions are evidenced in actions. Decisions live in duty.

- Patriots are students of history actively engaged in the present, who protect and defend the principles of freedom upon which the country was founded. They embrace responsibility and build on behalf of future generations. They sacrifice to ensure liberty. These citizens are the guarantors of the rights we hold dear. These people assure that the United States of America remains a strong and sovereign land.

Chapter 1
The Leader's View of History

Fourscore and seven years ago...

Gentle rhythms and compelling cadences marked the words of the Gettysburg Address, molding beauty with intentionality and thoughtful expression. Many orators of Lincoln's day, including politicians whom he influenced and those who impacted him, employed flowery, lofty expressions in their efforts to impress and sway their listeners. In fact, Lincoln himself often utilized similar techniques in many of his early political speeches.

Lincoln did it simpler at Gettysburg. Somehow in this short address, the president expressed his central and important themes quicker and more effectively. Maybe it was his humble upbringing, focused reading and studying, and impeccable logic that created unique mixtures of commonality and brilliance in this communication. Whatever the case, Lincoln's remarkable wisdom crafted what some would term a communication art form not surpassed since.

Was it effective? Yes. People remembered and acted upon what they heard, as future generations continue to do today.

Look again at that opening. Lincoln could have easily said "eighty-seven years ago," but the effect he created with "*fourscore and seven*" was elevating and inspirational. He set his content apart with phrases designed to make his audience contemplate their history.

Combining eloquent language with down to earth expression, he helped his audience recognize that, while he was a learned man, he had come *from* them. He could speak *to* them because he was one *of* them. The lesson is this: leaders who communicate effectively identify with their audience.

He was 51 years old when he was first elected president (November 6, 1860) and 52 years old when he began his first term (March 4, 1861). At the time of the Gettysburg Address, he was in his 54th year. His age, and the age of the country he led, were fairly close in proximity.

There were many people alive in 1863 whose fathers and grandfathers had contended in prior wars for the young nation. Memories were still fresh for the soldiers' families and the combatants of the nation's conflicts between 1775 and 1848: the Revolutionary War, the War of 1812 with Great Britain, and the Mexican-American War. Indeed, many soldiers wearing blue or gray during the Gettysburg conflict had known each other prior to the Civil War when they had fought on the same side for the United States.

The men and women who made up the armies of North and South, as well as Lincoln's audience, were bound to each other in time and place. The current population represented those who had survived and thrived through toil and test. These had paid the costs, had endured the sufferings, and had sacrificed much for their country's causes.

We know that the nation Lincoln sought to preserve would endure many more conflicts, but the people of Lincoln's era had no idea what was coming. At the time of the speech, the fate of the United States was in no way decided. On that November day in 1863, a dependable future was anything but secure for this fledging nation, still in its infancy when compared to the older empires of Europe, Asia, and the East.

In his opening phrase, President Lincoln anchored his hearers to a history that unified them. His words illustrated what all great leaders recognize—that history shapes us. Through declarations, decisions, acts, and consequences, a people—its cultures and world views—are molded and modeled.

Leaders set frameworks of understanding into which followers position themselves. Effective leaders help their followers frame choices against revealed and lasting truth.

Leaders don't change history—they learn from it. Then they teach the lessons of history to those who follow. Leaders possessing long-term views glean knowledge and wisdom from events and people who have lived before, educating from their experiences.

Consider what binds you to your past. Memory may be stimulated by photographs, medals, faded newspaper clippings, war records, songs, and stories related by the elderly. Preserving memories is important, regardless of the stages of life. Most interested persons reach a point where they *want* to know what has influenced them, including their ancestry and heritage.

The advent of photography in the 1800's, sound recordings and motion pictures in the 1900's, and digital technology in the 2000's have made archiving and retrieving information far easier and more durable. Nothing, however, takes the place of memory. When all is said and done it is living remembrance that motivates an individual to contemplate his or her past, dwell in the present, and look to the future.

When We Visited Gettysburg

Thoughts being formed may morph into firmly held opinions given the right stimulus, desire, circumstances, and proofs. Eventually convictions emerge. These become life lessons passed down from one generation to the next. Older generations hope that younger ones will build upon the learned truths of the past to be better positioned for application and instruction.

My son Justin and I visited Gettysburg in celebration of my son's 16th birthday. It was a remarkable and wonderful trip, forever etched in our memories. It was a time of inspiration, instruction, and investment. We were there to have a great time and to learn the life lessons that resounded from 1863 to the present.

While we did many of the things tourists do, we were also on a mission: We wanted to honor the soldiers who had fought and died on this battlefield. We wanted to observe their history and understand their motives and methods. This trip composed more than a pleasurable pastime for father and son. This was a time for appreciating sacrifice.

When one gives his or her life for the benefit of another, that gift represents a payment of immense value in exchange for additional untold values on behalf of those who receive. My son and I sought to embrace and understand monumental and sacred acts of giving, not only from those who fought in and around the small town in 1863, but for those who continue to fight for the freedoms we hold dear, when and wherever duty calls.

A leader's view of history considers and profoundly appreciates the contributions of those who pay it forward on behalf of others. What is cherished today is often composed of what was given up yesterday.

We spent a week wandering the battle's grounds. We drove the Gettysburg National Military Park Auto Tour. Independently we hiked up Little Round Top, explored Devil's Den, the Wheatfield, Rose Farm, and the Peach Orchard, and walked the open fields of Pickett's Charge—from both directions.

We viewed the expanses from Oak Hill and Oak Ridge and imagined the troops' movements in and around the grounds of the McPherson Farm and the historic McPherson barn which stands to this day. We meandered throughout the town, visited Culp's Farm and Culp's Hill, Spangler's Spring, Evergreen Cemetery, the Gettysburg National Cemetery, and Cemetery Hill. We drove and hiked Seminary Ridge, rested under the trees by the Lutheran Theological Seminary, and bicycled on the roads that traverse the open fields.

We compared era photos with modern ones. We gained a perspective of what it meant to preserve the past for this generation and those to come. In this realization we achieved a broader *depth* of understanding. Activities of tremendous significance had occurred here. This ground had been set apart.

We soon recognized a simple but profound truth: we are better today for what occurred in Gettysburg in July and November of 1863. And we were grateful.

Leaders observe and weigh history carefully. Life truths emerge from the lessons history teaches for those who appreciate and apply what they learn.

Wise leaders do not discard the past. They combine history's enduring principles, those for which heroes lived and died, into the causes their current stages of life require. They remember that decisions of their forebears rested upon the lasting truths *their* predecessors employed. Each generation builds upon the foundations of their ancestors.

We can do nothing less than emulate this model. We must teach what we learn to those who follow us.

Chapter 2
Strong Foundations

...our fathers brought forth on this continent, a new nation, conceived in Liberty, and dedicated to the proposition that all men are created equal.

Effective leaders purposefully construct their legacies upon foundations of enduring truth. Legacies that matter last beyond personalities, contributions, even organizations.

Legacy-driven leaders recognize that greatness resides less on the person and more on the process of contribution of which they are a part. These pacesetters possess a profound understanding of history, an awareness of current events, and a vision of what can be when positive principles are correctly applied into action.

Lincoln thought highly of the Declaration of Independence. As the newly elected president traveling to Washington, D.C. for his inauguration, he spoke in Philadelphia at Independence Hall on February 22, 1861: *"I have never had a feeling politically that did not spring from the sentiments embodied in the Declaration of Independence."*

Lincoln referred to a profound principle:

> *"...something in that Declaration giving liberty, not alone to the people of this country, but hope to the world for all future time. It was that which gave promise that in due time the weights should be lifted from the shoulders of all men, and that all should have an equal chance. This is the sentiment embodied in that Declaration of Independence."*

He aligned with that document's sustainable, protecting, life-giving truths. He based his conclusions about the resilience of the United States squarely on the immovable principles it contained.

He knew his responsibility was not to reinvent or reinterpret what the Declaration said, but instead to implement its doctrines no matter the cost. History would demonstrate that he died in his quest to state and activate the truths embedded in the document's enduring language.

Today the Declaration of Independence can be viewed in the Rotunda for the Charters of Freedom at the National Archives in Washington, D.C. Those who stop to ponder the parchment and what it says cannot help but be impressed. Often they are inspired beyond words.

This document announced independence. It defined the reasons behind the steps the young nation was choosing to take, to sever itself from its mother country.

The men who signed the parchment could very likely imagine the costs to be paid for their allegiance to the truths the declaration articulated. Theirs was a cause untried, an experiment in self governing that, if it succeeded, would give rise to *"the last, best hope of earth"*—a phrase Lincoln coined in correspondence to Congress on December 1, 1862. The framers and signers of the declaration had concluded their document with these words: "And for the support of this declaration, with a firm reliance on the protection of Divine Providence, we mutually pledge to each other our lives, our fortunes and our sacred honor." For the cause in which they believed they depended on God, they were fully engaged, and firmly committed.

A proposition is defined as "something offered for consideration or acceptance" according to *Merriam-Webster's 11th Collegiate Dictionary*. The proposition Lincoln quoted in the speech, "...that all men are created equal..." rested on an inviolate principle. It is this: all human beings possess identical God-given attributes. One is the equality of every individual.

Leaders build for their day and others' futures by resting thoughts and actions upon solid principles like this one. At a time when the phrase "all men are created equal" was sorely tried, tested, and often denied, Lincoln refused these objections. He remained true to the immovable truth of equality. The importance of this proposition included the acknowledgement that adherence to this or any foundational principle may indeed include tough choices and ultimate sacrifice.

Clearly the Civil War constituted the severest test to the internal resilience of the United States since its founding. Would it survive?

In January of 1838 Lincoln spoke to The Young Men's Lyceum in Springfield, Illinois. His speech was entitled "The Perpetuation of Our Political Institutions." In this oration, Lincoln expressed his confidence in the strength of the Union through observance of its laws. He also accurately predicted the conditions of the nation's downfall were it ever to occur.

At the time of the Lyceum speech he was 28 years of age. This oration would be remarkable if it were written by an older and highly educated person. It was all the more so coming from a young man, a so-called uneducated backwoodsman.

Enjoy, admire, and learn from its greatness as you read these lines.

> *"...At what point shall we expect the approach of danger? By what means shall we fortify against it?—Shall we expect some transatlantic military giant, to step the Ocean, and crush us at a blow? Never!—All the armies of Europe, Asia and Africa combined, with all the treasure of the earth (our own excepted) in their military chest; with a Bonaparte for a commander, could not by force, take a drink from the Ohio, or make a track on the Blue Ridge, in a trial of a thousand years.*
>
> *At what point then is the approach of danger to be expected? I answer, if it ever reach us, it must spring up amongst us. It cannot come from abroad. If destruction be our lot, we must ourselves be its author and finisher. As a nation of freemen, we must live through all time, or die by suicide...*
>
> *...Let every American, every lover of liberty, every well wisher to his posterity, swear by the blood of the Revolution, never to violate in the least particular, the laws of the country; and never to tolerate their violation by others. As the patriots of seventy-six did to the support of the Declaration of Independence, so*

> *to the support of the Constitution and Laws, let every American pledge his life, his property, and his sacred honor;—let every man remember that to violate the law, is to trample on the blood of his father, and to tear the character of his own, and his children's liberty. Let reverence for the laws, be breathed by every American mother, to the lisping babe, that prattles on her lap—let it be taught in schools, in seminaries, and in colleges; let it be written in Primers, spelling books, and in Almanacs;—let it be preached from the pulpit, proclaimed in legislative halls, and enforced in courts of justice. And, in short, let it become the political religion of the nation; and let the old and the young, the rich and the poor, the grave and the gay, of all sexes and tongues, and colors and conditions, sacrifice unceasingly upon its altars."*

In every era the United States has faced threats to liberty from foreign lands, leaders, or ideologies. Though severely assaulted, this country has survived and thrived. However, it remains true that if destruction or dissolution should ever come, it will emerge from within us.

Legacy-driven leaders anchor their decisions and actions on solid fundamentals. They become acutely aware of the dangers their organizations face whether threats come from without or fester from within. These leaders teach their followers to be vigilant. They preserve what they hold dear and persevere to secure the futures they desire.

Leadership's legacies last beyond what is expedient. They rest upon enduring principle, not endless opinion. Committed people lead with confidence coming from truth. Followers align with what they are convinced is right.

What viable and lasting principles does your leadership depend upon and incorporate? The value of human life and the dignity of the individual may be two examples. Sacrifice for a higher and worthy cause may be one more. Giving to someone without desiring recognition, yet another.

Expediency and convenience shun endurance, as do lying and manipulation. For great leaders awareness of contemporary and passing ideological fads does not determine whether a course may be right or wrong.

Vision about what should be achieved will be driven by principles that rise above circumstances. Often this vision changes the circumstances it confronts. This vision will not be denied. This vision faces difficulties with assurance and fortitude so that no matter the degrees of negativism victories will be won. Ideology and practices worth preserving will thrive.

Circumstantial change may bow to whims. However, principle-based leaders decide and dwell in practices composed of far more than surface, people-pleasing proclamations along with their accompanying unfulfilled promises. Shallow pledges may win elections. Upon more thorough investigation, however, they do not endure the supreme tests and testimonies of time.

If you are the leader, build on strong foundations, proven to be true. Your leadership contributions will outlast you, as they should.

Chapter 3
Crises

Now we are engaged in a great civil war, testing whether that nation, or any nation so conceived and so dedicated, can long endure. We are met on a great battlefield of that war.

Crises cannot be shunned. While conflict should be avoided if possible, it must never be ignored to the degree of replacing conviction with complacency, freedom with bondage, or commitment with apathy.

Crises are tests. They come with amazing frequency. Some are anticipated, but many appear without warning. Problems, regardless of source, are as sure as death, taxes, and tomorrow's rising sun.

Negative circumstances and malicious events, as bad as they may be, bear opportunities for creating and implementing positive and effective solutions—a good leader knows this. He or she searches for lasting resolutions. A great leader encourages his or her followers to do the same.

Methods chosen to solve problems are decisions birthed from values and borne on desired behaviors. A collection of these behaviors is known as a value system. The behaviors described within the system are learned through education, honed through experience, and practiced in virtually all the environments of life.

Value systems are evidenced in actions. Motives precede movements, creeds come before deeds, decisions pre-exist functions. A value system describes behaviors that originate from a world view no matter where it came from or how it developed.

Effective leaders respect and seek to advance uplifting values-driven behaviors, especially in times of crisis. They endeavor to model and teach these preferred actions to those who follow.

One collection of desired behaviors is "The Twelve Laws of Understanding," quoted from *Leadership Is—How to Build Your Legacy*.

Twelve Laws of Understanding

- Realize I am responsible for my own choices, not others'; that changing someone else's behavior is not my responsibility; rather, I need to change me.
- Seek to understand how the other person thinks and communicates; use his or her language.
- Model what I want.
- Set realistic limits on what is acceptable behavior.
- Impose these limits on myself, first.
- Desire the best, but prepare for difficulty; seek creative, peaceful solutions.
- Seek and pray for wisdom.
- Remember, at the right times.
- Encourage always.
- Think first, listen most, and speak seldom.
- Realize growth involves change, change can mean pain, and patience on the journey is a virtue.
- Love. Establish meaningful relationships.

Law #6 states, "Desire the best, but prepare for difficulty; seek creative, peaceful solutions." There is no substitute for an earnest desire for positive outcomes to difficult problems. This desire, however, does not always produce this result. Leaders remain aware that negatives sometimes accompany the best-intentioned efforts, and they prepare for this eventuality.

The events at Fort Sumter beginning on April 10, 1861 present a graphic illustration of Lincoln's desire for a peaceful resolution to a thorny situation. The fort was a United States garrison located on a sandbar in the Charleston Harbor. The Union soldiers stationed there needed supplies. Lincoln decided to provision them. Amid these efforts the South opened fire on April 12 and the war began. While there were no casualties from the 34-hour bombardment, the symbolism to the North and the South was immense. The division was real, the conflict of separation unavoidable. Thoughts and plans for peace completely evaporated.

Crises come and go as do the responses to address them. Responses reflect the values engaged parties believe in and strive to uphold. In all cases great leaders seek to fully understand the nature of the problems and to deal with them based on what they believe is right.

Lincoln's words in this portion of the Gettysburg Address accurately portray three vital aspects of dealing with monumental conflict: composition, time, and location.

The first can be found in the phrase *"so conceived and so dedicated."* The make-up of an organization often determines how its difficulties are identified and treated. The composition of the Union compelled its constitutional adherents to honor what every state had agreed to uphold upon entering the United States. Each had agreed to belong to a nation united under one Federal Government, designed to exist in perpetuity.

Composition and dedication are embodied in the word united. The implied and expressed truth is this: No division, regardless of the degrees of disagreement that may pervade its history, could ever serve to sever the unity of the nation.

A framework had been constructed in which conflict would have to be resolved, no matter what. The alternative, completely unacceptable, would mean a disintegration of the very tenets upon which the nation was founded. Disintegration would mean the replacement of the designed and desirable system with a markedly imperfect one.

Next, a true sense of time cannot be ignored. Look closely at the phrase *"can long endure."* To endure is to outlast the odds no matter their degrees of difficulty. Circumstances notwithstanding, the nation had been destined to stand.

Permanence was not optional. Everyone knew that struggles would come and go in their own era. Most believed that the nation would survive if it never let go of its values.

Lincoln was tenacious. He desired the national unity to

be restored. He was willing to commit the effort, energy, and resources to accomplish this goal.

Leaders work for endurance over the long haul. They know which battles are worth the fight, and which goals merit sacrifice. This means, of course, that some conflicts are not worth the effort or time that may have to be expended. Putting strengths and actions into those that demonstrate the greatest value are where victories of positive endurance live.

Third, location is often a determiner of winning or losing. Consider this sentence: "*We are met on a great battlefield of that war.*" Military strategists take varying factors into account when deciding on the location of a conflict, if the opportunity to choose a field is present.

According to my good friend, Major Kevin Bouren, United States Army:

> "No military commander wants to go into a fight at a disadvantage, or worse, with little chance of victory. To provide the greatest opportunity for mission accomplishment, commanders analyze several factors to help inform their situational understanding of an operation. From a strategic standpoint, Army doctrine teaches commanders to look at the mission, enemy, terrain and weather, troops and support available, time available, and civil

considerations (we use the acronym METT-TC). This analysis will largely determine how—and whether—the commander will pursue that fight. Once the commander decides to go with the mission, he uses tactical considerations such as cover and concealment, key and decisive terrain, fields of fire, man-made or natural obstacles, and avenues of approach. To poise his unit for success, the commander does the hard work and the due diligence to find the most advantageous location to position his forces. Critical to the commander's overall assessment is using good judgment informed by experience to ensure his forces have occupied a position that also provides flexibility to adjust during the fight. In the end, commanders want their unit to emerge victorious and be ready for the follow-on mission."

How a leader chooses to deal with crises includes determining a proper location. Some historians consider the fields and town of Gettysburg to be battlegrounds that were decided accidentally. Consider these facts: The town was strategic for many reasons. Both armies recognized this soon after they discovered each other's positions. Ten roads intersected the town's limits. It was a communication hub and a transportation link. Its location was an asset for the movements of war, as well as a tie for commerce in times of peace. These factors proved to be decisive for the battle the town eventually bore.

If you are the leader, consider where you choose to wage your battles. The wise leader recognizes that conflicts will be fought; the effective leader chooses where problems should be dealt with. He or she picks a favorable location for engagement if that choice is possible. That choice often affects how problematic issues are handled.

A conscientious student of Gettysburg and Lincoln's leadership learns how to best address the difficulties that are sure to come. This student considers composition, time, and location, aware that all three elements are vital to success.

Because challenges can't and won't be denied, the better leader faces them with knowledge, wisdom, and courage. Fortitude emerges from the values that bind the leader and the followers to their cause. Victory may well be within their grasp when factors within their control are brought to bear on the problems that must be solved.

Chapter 4
Sacrifice

We have come to dedicate a portion of that field, as a final resting place for those who here gave their lives that that nation might live. It is altogether fitting and proper that we should do this.

Leaders who appreciate enduring principles understand the importance of remembrance and dedication. They consecrate times, places, and people who have given for the benefit of others. They honor and respect the individuals who have defended what they know is just and true.

This setting-apart cherishes the past, provisions the present, and frames the future. Memories of events and people are preserved as treasures. These memories create the curriculum and compose the classrooms for those who desire to learn what sacrifice really means.

A cemetery is a repository for the remains of those who have perished. In his speech, Lincoln chose the phrase *"a final resting place"* instead of the more common word, cemetery. Why? Perhaps it was because that location constituted more than a cemetery. Maybe it was that he considered the place to be sacred ground for the soldiers who died and were buried not far from where they fell.

Gettysburg comprises an immense battlefield. The vastness of the landscape reminds one of the larger panoramas of our lives, where struggles ensue and losses and gains compose the experiences of life. The Gettysburg National Military Park covers more than 6,000 acres alone. The sites of the three-day conflict consumed the town and surrounding areas in 1863, and they still do today.

The battlefield area encompasses numerous local roads, two state highways, three colleges, and a vast array of businesses. Tourists dining in local restaurants are often times overheard inquiring of a waiter where the battlefield is. The answer is "You're on it."

In 1863 the population numbered approximately 2,500. The battle brought an additional 165,000 persons, with 72,000 horses, along with winding and lengthy columns of war materiel, including ammunition caissons and wagons carrying mountains of supplies in support of two huge armies. This invasion of people and provisions bloated the town, straining its meager resources.

Lincoln may have seen some of the lingering effects of the battle, many of which can still easily be observed today. Buildings bear the marks of bullet holes, one of the most obvious being the Farnsworth House on Baltimore Street. Two sycamore trees across the street from the Farnsworth House were silent witnesses as Lincoln passed by on horseback on his way from the David Wills House to the cemetery to give the speech. At the base of one of these trees, a plaque has been placed which reads, in part, "President Lincoln passed by this tree on November 19, 1863."

Many other trees, called Witness Trees, remain from July 1, 2, and 3 of that year. May they continue to stand, almost 150 years after the battle.

The cupola of the Lutheran Theological Seminary was used by leaders of both armies—including Robert E. Lee—to observe troop movements during the ebb and flow of the conflict. The barn of the Trostle House displays the hole of a Confederate cannon ball. The barn of the McPherson Farm, the copse of trees, the George Weikert Farm, and the massive outcroppings of Devil's Den and Little Round Top stand guard.

Other rocks—especially the large ones—silently echo

their recollections. So many battle era photos include them. These stones are poignant reminders of the conflict, especially when viewed through the excellent collections of old and modern photography and associated written descriptions by William Frassanito. I heartily recommend Frassanito's books, *Gettysburg: A Journey in Time*; *Early Photography at Gettysburg*; *Gettysburg, Then & Now: Touring the Battlefield With Old Photos*; *The Gettysburg Then and Now Companion*; and *The Gettysburg Bicentennial Album*.

Millions of people have visited Gettysburg since July of 1863. Remarkably, much of the battlefield remains largely unmarred. Efforts of many groups, including the National Park Service, have preserved the surroundings, sacred to the memories of those who fought and perished there.

Over a thousand monuments and memorials are located throughout the battlefield area. Reverence should accompany observing them.

Carved stones do not recall life. Yet their inscriptions ask us to pause and reflect. If we care about honor, courage, belief, and giving on behalf of others, we will stop, learn, and remember with respect.

Lincoln's remarks were heard by people who had witnessed the battle. Scars from its calamity of death were still fresh in the minds of many of his listeners. They remembered. So should we. History teaches contemporary and future generations the awesome responsibilities that accompany acts of remembering.

One responsibility is to embrace and emulate tenets of exemplary leadership. We can learn much from studying Lincoln's approach to difficult circumstances.

When he delivered the Gettysburg Address, considerations of war were on the forefront of everyone's minds. We can only imagine the thoughts that permeated the president's being as he stood on the platform to deliver the speech.

So much had transpired that had given birth to the clarity of his communication. Unbeknownst to Lincoln and his audience were the events of history still to be written; these would include a second presidential election and his assassination.

As noted in *Industrial Strength Solutions*, pages 18 and 19:

> "During 1862, at a height of profound discouragement for the Union in America's Civil War, President Abraham Lincoln was faced with the awesome consideration of weighing mounting and incredible costs of lives sacrificed and property decimated on both sides. The results he and the country endured appeared at that time to be far from justified or satisfactory; indeed, they were at many

moments monumentally discouraging beyond words. A victory for the Union seemed distant at best. It was during these forlorn and lonely seasons for the president, as defeat upon defeat converged from multiple sources, that Lincoln made insurmountably tough decisions. He had to. His choices would make or break not only the conduct of the war, but ultimately determine the Union's success or failure. Criticism from within and conflict from without made his process of decision-making harder yet, but true greatness shone and he chose what he deemed best.

Upon his resolve to continue to move down the path he had selected, because he believed and declared he was acting as an instrument of the people to uphold the Constitution and save the Union, he enacted a war and humanitarian measure that forever put the blight of slavery on its path of eventual destruction. That measure was, of course, the Emancipation Proclamation. The Union armies could benefit from the manpower the emancipated slaves would provide, and the slaves that were freed were those who at that time were located in the States that had rebelled. Not ever referring to the Confederacy as a separate country, only as States 'then in rebellion' to the United States, he exercised his authority over and on behalf of the people held as slaves within those States, who, because of their freedom, helped the Union win the war and preserve the country from disastrous dissolution.

When Lincoln was assassinated it was said that the South lost one of its greatest supporters, and it was true, for as part of the plan to restore the Union, in addition to the Emancipation Proclamation, Lincoln had articulated in the weeks and days just before his death his desires to make the process of restoration and reconstruction as right and accessible for achievement as possible. To empower the States that had rebelled to rejoin the Union, Lincoln was not in favor of burdening them with unnecessary measures born of a spirit of vindictiveness or punitive subjugation; rather, he asked only for fundamental requirements needed as basis points to unify the country in the short term and reinstate the States for a United States that would endure in perpetuity.

As he closed his Second Inaugural address,

delivered on March 4, 1865, he proclaimed these words, 'With malice toward none; with charity for all; with firmness in the right, as God gives us to see the right, let us strive on to finish the work we are in; to bind up the nation's wounds; to care for him who shall have borne the battle, and for his widow, and his orphan—to do all which may achieve and cherish a just and lasting peace among ourselves, and with all nations.' These immortal words were addressed to a country that despaired of war and was desperate for peace, and they came at the time when Appomattox was still weeks away, but it was coming, and eventually did.

Some truths are worth believing, desiring, risking for, and acting upon. The union of the United States of America was certainly one of them. The union, or perhaps better put, the unification coming from essential agreement on values, goals, people, process and product may be representative of other more contemporary causes. These considerations, while not requiring the extent of a sacrifice of civil war, may inspire courage and boldness based on right attitudes and attributes that will encourage people who agree to engage in right actions to produce better results than the status quo, especially if the status quo is not producing well, or if people on teams in your organization are involved in their own uncivil wars."

Great leadership confronts negatives with positive principles and practices. The stronger the conflict, the more resilient the dedication must be to pursue right action, regardless of cost.

Leaders understand this maxim: Truths worthy of belief and sacrifice are rehearsed and applied despite pain and adverse circumstances. Core principles and practices affect all they touch in every era and location.

Superb leaders are fully aware that attacks on right action never cease, that negativity comes in a myriad of ways. Some blows are born of words. Others are demonstrated in deeds.

Enduring leaders know that criticism doesn't make or mold character. Destructive commentary and conflict reveal a leader's inborn strengths held in reserve. Positive contributions originating from adherence to right values come to the forefront when the needs become known and the timing is right.

One of the most powerful letters ever given in defense of responsible action was Abraham Lincoln's reply to Horace

Greeley. On August 19, 1862 Mr. Greeley, editor of the *New York Tribune*, published an open letter to the president in the form of an editorial entitled *The Prayer of Twenty Millions*. In this letter Greeley intimated that Lincoln's administration was floundering, purposeless, on the war.

Lincoln responded to Greeley on August 22, 1862, as follows:

> *Executive Mansion,*
> *Washington, August 22, 1862.*
>
> *Hon. Horace Greeley:*
> *Dear Sir.*
>
> *I have just read yours of the 19th. addressed to myself through the New-York Tribune. As to the policy I "seem to be pursuing" as you say, I have not meant to leave any one in doubt.*
>
> *I would save the Union. I would save it the shortest way under the Constitution. The sooner the national authority can be restored; the nearer the Union will be "the Union as it was." If there be those who would not save the Union, unless they could at the same time save slavery, I do not agree with them. If there*

be those who would not save the Union unless they could at the same time destroy slavery, I do not agree with them. My paramount object in this struggle is to save the Union, and is not either to save or to destroy slavery. If I could save the Union without freeing any slave I would do it, and if I could save it by freeing all the slaves I would do it; and if I could save it by freeing some and leaving others alone I would also do that. What I do about slavery, and the colored race, I do because I believe it helps to save the Union; and what I forbear, I forbear because I do not believe it would help to save the Union. I shall do less whenever I shall believe what I am doing hurts the cause, and I shall do more whenever I shall believe doing more will help the cause. I shall try to correct errors when shown to be errors; and I shall adopt new views so fast as they shall appear to be true views.

I have here stated my purpose according to my view of official duty; and I intend no modification of my oft-expressed personal wish that all men everywhere could be free.

Yours,
A. Lincoln.

Delineating single focus points was one of Lincoln's true strengths. Let's learn from him.

Consider these questions if you are the leader: To what degree do your followers know exactly what you stand for? How committed are you to dedicate yourself to your followers' successes, supporting them in spite of what it may cost? How do your followers' actions demonstrate firm resolve especially in the tough times? How much would you and your followers be willing to sacrifice to uphold what you are convinced is true?

When you and the people you lead showcase solid agreement on right principles, you can face onslaughts together and overcome problems that must be confronted. This is one vital characteristic of a strong and enduring organization.

If you are the leader, follow the example of Lincoln. Dedicate yourself to your followers and consecrate your actions for their wellbeing. It is fitting and proper that you should do this.

Declare what you want by demonstrating it through your words and actions. This dedication will set you and your followers apart to achieve meritorious results no matter the degrees of sacrifice required.

Chapter 5
Limits

But, in a larger sense, we cannot dedicate—we cannot consecrate—we cannot hallow—this ground. The brave men, living and dead, who struggled here, have consecrated it, far above our poor power to add or detract. The world will little note, nor long remember what we say here, but it can never forget what they did here.

Lincoln sincerely believed, and sometimes expressed, that his words were less than adequate or might not be memorable. While he was correct in many positions, thankfully he was wrong in this conclusion.

It is true that words alone, even great ones, may not carry the weight of the deeds that precede or follow them. It may be impossible to predict the effects of proclamations of notable men and women as their words are spoken.

Expressions become memorable and endure not because of language alone. Attending circumstances, residual effects, historical reminiscences, and momentous events often infuse meaning into what has been said and provide contexts in which words ring true.

Lincoln's words still speak, and in this section of the Gettysburg Address another leadership principle is revealed: Leaders recognize their limits. They understand what is and what is not within their control. They appreciate and willingly submit to "a larger sense."

Appropriately responding to limits raises an important distinction between superior and inferior leadership. Leaders who know and understand their limits reveal higher degrees of maturity and wisdom as they deal with the challenges they face. How they handle what they don't know is as important as how they handle what they do know.

Lincoln realized that his understanding of the Gettysburg battle could not equate to that of a soldier who had struggled or died on that field. He was wise to recognize that there were some shoes he could not fill.

The president's tribute in these lines was not self-deprecating. Rather, his comments appropriately positioned and honored the soldiers who had sanctified the battleground with their blood.

Only those so engaged could completely do what the speeches of the day were designed to do: consecrate the ground and preserve the memory and the meaning of the place. Only those who were present and had endured the battle could correctly position the combatant for recognition above any eloquence of verbal expression.

History would show that Lincoln's words would live alongside the memories of fallen soldiers and the honors rightly bestowed upon them. Learn and embrace this truth: Lasting legacies are born and flourish when right communication, core principles, and concrete actions cooperate.

Era photos taken shortly after the battle, beginning on July 5, 1863, poignantly relate scenes of destruction and death. We don't know if Lincoln had seen any of these photos before he delivered his address.

However, when today's observer combines the old camera views with Lincoln's living words, this alignment fashions profound effects. It can cause the student of the battle and Lincoln's leadership to reflect on issues of life and death more intentionally. It can help the learner appreciate sacrifices more carefully, confront seemingly insurmountable odds with additional fortitude, and to more firmly commit to building a future of liberty and freedom for those who are yet to come.

Most casual tourists visiting Gettysburg possess little

idea of what they are looking at apart from signage or photo recognition. One cannot be casual about this place, however, when one considers the immense payments made on these fields and in these forests by the soldiers who struggled there.

In a larger sense, discovering the exact spots of soldiers' deaths or locating the strategic placements of men and materiel can become a contribution in a composition of the sacred. For the dedicated observer, these places become far more than sites to observe and photograph. These locations are transformed into altars of gratitude, sites set apart as holy.

Viewpoints of one generation teach lessons from the past and assist leaders to apply principles in the present. The confines and perspectives of *now* carry limits for everyone. Yet, they also beget motives for adopting values-driven duties that will affect the people and events of tomorrow.

Leaders remember that positive results occur when enduring right and preferred principles are embraced and practiced. The Law of Sowing and Reaping and the Law of Compensation are in play here: Every action bears a reaction; each cause births an effect.

There is no substitute for proper consecration of hallowed ground. All people should appreciate the sacrifices of their forebears.

Yet it is for us to learn, forecast, and prepare. We must

set in motion right actions designed to produce beneficial outcomes lest the lessons of history remain impotent.

Leaders who build legacy recognize their limits and honor the greatness that has preceded them. They consecrate the payments of former generations as they provide a context for current contributions. These leaders diligently prepare their followers for future successes that will exceed what today's leaders are capable of providing.

This is what Lincoln did. It is what we should do, also.

Effects endure beyond the events that give them life.
Learn their truths.
History's lessons shape the minds and means of generations.

Chapter 6
Unfinished Work

It is for us the living, rather, to be dedicated here to the unfinished work which they who fought here have thus far so nobly advanced. It is rather for us to be here dedicated to the great task remaining before us—

Responsibilities rest upon the living. They must complete what those who have died cannot. Those alive today possess obligations to build upon the legacies passed down from their ancestors and, in light of these legacies, to construct transferable inheritances of their own.

Lincoln understood the sacrifices of his forebears. He was well acquainted with the history of the nation he led. He valued the challenges his predecessors had confronted and the victories they had won. His solemn constitutional pledge was to restore and preserve the Union the founding fathers had created. His dedication to fulfill this task was unwavering, though that commitment would eventually cost his life and the lives of 600,000 other brave Americans in the brutal combat, disease, and cruel aftermaths of the Civil War.

Every generation should consider the contributions of those who have gone before. Each generation lives with the results of a past generation's decisions, good or bad. Choices remain for a current population to learn from its past, build upon it, and pass along something better to those who will come after.

Honorable men and women comprehend and appreciate the worth of enduring beliefs, living traditions, and acts of sacrifice. Opinion is molded and culture is shaped by these elements of constitution. Gifts from history remind the folks of today that they must protect and advance the creeds and deeds that withstand the onslaughts of time.

Each generation must work to guarantee freedom's rights and privileges, making them available to the people of tomorrow. The responsibilities of constructing and living out positive legacies are never done, nor should they be. There is work to do for all who take up the mantles of their teachers and leaders. There are great tasks remaining. What one generation may not complete, the next must strive to fulfill.

In a vibrant and productive environment, students become teachers and followers grow into leaders: this cycle is continuous. Teachers and leaders who generate living legacies create opportunities for successors to take their places and accomplish more.

Contributing in excess of what is inherited moves people to invest for tomorrow. Without this focus a generation stagnates and lives upon the successes or failures of a former time and place.

Purposeful investors are builders for more than their day. These people see beyond their era. They construct success frameworks for generations yet unborn.

People alive today will be unacquainted with succeeding generations a hundred years hence. True investors provide benefits they will never enjoy to individuals they will never know.

Greatness does not reside exclusively in today's accomplishments, as important as they may be. Defining moments of greatness reside in the formation of unshakable foundations upon which people yet unborn can construct even more substantial and beneficial contributions to the human heart, soul, mind, and wellbeing.

People who think and act this way are trendsetters. They emulate the examples of Lincoln and other superior leaders who have made positive and indelible marks on history. These people make a difference.

Here is another central truth: The admirable works of one generation are finished well when their leaders prepare those who follow to succeed at greater levels than the current generation. Gifts of living contributors must surpass the inheritance of their predecessors. This broader construct begs for more desirable and long lasting results than contemporary generations are capable of.

An enduring and growing legacy begins as a seed that is planted by a visionary into the fertile soil of another's life. With care and cultivation that seed develops and matures. Nurtured over time it provides a harvest of substantially more than a one-to-one return.

This harvest may include ultimate sacrifice. In war or in peace, in struggle or in ease, the death of one may guarantee the life of the other. "Greater love hath no man than this, that a man lay down his life for his friends." (John 15:13, KJV).

Investments like these look beyond convenience to continuance. They help followers and students fulfill more than what is expected today to achieve even greater abundance tomorrow.

Diligent followers embrace the unfinished works of their leaders and complete them. This is called finishing. Responsible people take up the challenge and do their part.

To build an enduring legacy some of these people surpass finishing. They mold frameworks in which others can contribute and through which succeeding generations can achieve even greater success than theirs. This is called finishing *well.*

The goal for dedicated leaders and followers, devoted teachers and students, is never just to finish. The goal is to finish well.

What is the unfinished work of those who have gone before you? How are you finishing the tasks they initiated? How well are you fulfilling and exceeding the results of the past while building for the future? What kinds of investments are you making for those who will come after you?

Climb the steps of the small hill, a part of Little Round Top, upon which the monument erected to the 20th Maine rests. This stone edifice marks the place where the flag was planted by Joshua Chamberlin's men. The location of the "colors" was a rallying point. It was a marker of offense, defense, and defiance to the enemy. The colors represented the lofty standards that bound dedicated people together to accomplish their mission amid overwhelming obstacles.

We could refer to the colors as eternally abiding principles and practices living generations uphold in sacrifice, perseverance, and devotion. Their truths are passed down to teach and encourage future men and women, preparing them to accomplish what remains to be done.

Another principle emerges: Examples of purposeful

dedication today become the permanent history lessons of tomorrow. It's an important truth.

The mandate for us, the living, is to take seriously what we learn, value, and offer. We want to finish the tasks remaining before us. We want those who follow us to be inspired by our contributions. We want them to complete our unfinished work and accomplish more than we could possibly imagine or provide.

Chapter 7
Increased Devotion

...that from these honored dead we take increased devotion to that cause for which they gave the last full measure of devotion—that we here highly resolve that these dead shall not have died in vain—

Many times I have stood alone and in silence at the copse of trees on Cemetery Ridge. This was the focal point established by General Robert E. Lee for Pickett's Charge on July 3, 1863. It is often called the High Water Mark of the Rebellion.

I've walked there in a blinding evening's snowstorm where my tracks in drifts of white composed the only tokens of my presence. I've been there in the lingering heat of a summer's night as gentle winds blew and whispered through the spreading branches of those trees. I have visited this place after the milling crowds of tourists have long since departed.

When I am there by myself I am able to concentrate better. I appreciate and enjoy the moments free of distraction.

Solitude frames the backdrop for deep and contemplative thought. Engaging in solitude is not an action many choose in our postmodern era, where expansive media continually bombard us and intrusive noise unceasingly surrounds us.

However, when the self-control of solitude is achieved, vistas of truth open up that otherwise may not be revealed. Enlivened and explorative thinking can result.

Solitude is a discipline. Serious students of principled truth do well to embrace and engage in it more often.

In those quiet moments, standing and gazing at those trees, I've often wondered what drove the men from both sides to sacrifice so much in that place and time. Certainly a resolute belief in their cause and the courage to defend it motivated them on one level. We also know that some of the soldiers fought for the thrill, and that others, duty bound, were resigned to the fact that they could die. Many did.

A perspective on where a person fits into the bigger picture may dictate how their contributions will be fulfilled. How many of those young men who fought at Gettysburg truly understood the stakes? Could they have had any idea of the importance of what they were doing and how their actions would be viewed by future generations?

Part of the reason they committed themselves to the conflict and an uncertain future may have been the experience and charisma of the leaders whom they followed. These leaders had proven themselves in prior wars. It must have been an honor to align with them.

At times of immense importance or within moments of fearful and unknown consequences, followers may literally move forward blindly, bound to obedience and duty. Trusting, they may endure epochal travail simply because a proven leader says, "Go."

Respect and admiration for leadership, as well as cause, country, and duty, may indeed compel men and women to willingly sacrifice all they have. Here's the lesson: People act out of desire when they are convinced of the truth of the leader's words, his or her character, and the viability of the cause the leader represents. Followers comply when they are sure what and whom they are obeying are right.

Lincoln referred to those who had given their all as honored. He respected them for who they were as well as for what they had done. Herein rests another leadership maxim: Leaders notice and praise the people who serve on behalf of a greater cause while recognizing and rewarding their deeds. They openly appreciate the persons *and* their contributions.

Leadership bears tremendous responsibility when it requests or requires followers to perform acts that define sacrifice. Degrees of devotion are carefully considered, and they should be.

Lincoln's use of the phrase *increased devotion* causes us to look closer at what he meant. There is a difference between devotion and *increased* devotion.

Devotion is dedicated motion toward an agreed, desired, and cooperative end. *Increased* devotion connotes a higher level of chosen obligation. It goes beyond what is expected. Increased devotion comprises extended commitment to bear any losses required to achieve a more enduring result for an even greater good.

Heroes are revealed in severely trying times. Brave individuals rise to points of unheard-of contributions when moments of expanded courage and strength are required. The full extent of their honorable character may be unknown before a major crisis engulfs them. Brutal difficulties may provide the opportunities for them to show their true composition.

The greatest degree of devotion, or as Lincoln put it, "*the last full measure of devotion,*" defines an ultimate sacrifice for a cause that remains beyond its conflict. The significance of a purpose upon which an individual stakes claim, name, and reputation makes up the reason for giving the last full measure. One so committed is a hero.

On one level Lincoln was referring to the fallen soldiers

at Gettysburg when he uttered the words we are considering. Notice, however, that he wasn't only talking about those who had died even though they were the centerpiece of his presentation. He was also referencing the living, those who would take up the cause and complete it.

What motivates a person to fulfill a challenging task? What births increased devotion when the stakes are highest? What causes one to *resolve* to finish well no matter what?

Often people look to those who have left their blood on a battlefield for the inspiration to keep going, to refuse to give up or give in. Others look to leaders they admire, receiving strength from their examples.

Lincoln's resolve concerned matters of life and death for individuals and a nation. The future of this country was at stake along with the lives, fortunes, and sacred honors of the people engaged in the struggle for a unified United States.

The phrase *highly resolve* denoted action that would contain a no-holds-barred dedication. The phrase implied that nothing would be held in reserve, that duty would be exercised to the bitter end.

Vain efforts produce mediocre contributions. They originate from lukewarm people of soft backbone and milk toast attitudes. These people fade and falter when sacrifice is required.

Gain efforts require more. Contributors possessing

a motive and a matching commitment are duty-bound achievers. They do not back down.

People so dedicated count the costs. Then they make definitive decisions. They seize opportunity. These people never quit until their jobs are done. They practice perseverance.

Individuals who demonstrate higher resolve display unadulterated alignment and adherence to principles that can never be released or traded away. They are men and women of fortitude. They uphold the causes for which they live with all the efforts they can give.

The leadership demonstrated by General Dwight D. Eisenhower is a prime example. On June 6, 1944, World War II began coming to an end in Europe. The general presented his Order of the Day: 6 June 1944. It read as follows:

> Soldiers, Sailors and Airmen of the Allied Expeditionary Force!
>
> You are about to embark upon the Great Crusade, toward which we have striven these many months. The eyes of the world are upon you. The hopes and prayers of liberty-loving people everywhere march with you. In company with our brave Allies and brothers-in-arms on other Fronts, you will bring about

the destruction of the German war machine, the elimination of Nazi tyranny over the oppressed peoples of Europe, and security for ourselves in a free world.

Your task will not be an easy one. Your enemy is well trained, well equipped and battle hardened. He will fight savagely.

But this is the year 1944! Much has happened since the Nazi triumphs of 1940-41. The United Nations have inflicted upon the Germans great defeats, in open battle, man-to-man. Our air offensive has seriously reduced their strength in the air and their capacity to wage war on the ground. Our Home Fronts have given us an overwhelming superiority in weapons and munitions of war, and placed at our disposal great reserves of trained fighting men. The tide has turned! The free men of the world are marching together to Victory!

I have full confidence in your courage and devotion to duty and skill in battle. We will accept nothing less than full Victory!

> Good luck! And let us beseech the blessing of Almighty God upon this great and noble undertaking.
>
> SIGNED: Dwight D. Eisenhower

Note this: Increased devotion initiates cooperation from people who agree on the merits of an endeavor. When they agree and are committed to fulfillment they contribute whatever it takes to make a worthy goal come true.

Lincoln believed that the deaths of honored soldiers would be validated in the lives of future generations. He desired that the legacies of the fallen would endure beyond the conflicts of his day. He was convinced that America was worth saving for all time. Foresight and devotion like this are characteristics of strong and effective leadership.

In 2009, a book of inspirational poetry was released entitled *Freedom Light—Expressions of Hope and Evidence*. Incorporated into the collection of verses is a song, "Keep the Dream Alive," which provides an illustration of increased devotion. Perhaps the piece will resonate with you.

Here's the bottom line: When a dream is worth a person's hope and desire, belief in its fulfillment generates action toward achievement. The dedication to make the dream come true is where resilience and perseverance dwell.

Lincoln's dream for the United States of America was for a unified nation, one that honored and adhered to its doctrines of independence and constitution. In this he never wavered.

How strong is your dream? What is your commitment to assure its fulfillment? The answers to these questions may consist in what you may be willing to sacrifice in order to make your dream become reality.

The dream you achieve may touch innumerable souls. For the good of yourself and the many, keep the dream alive.

Keep the Dream Alive

Keep the dream alive
In your heart, in your soul,
Don't give up on the prize,
Keep your eyes on the goal.

When the journey is true,
Then it's all up to you
To pursue, carry on,
It's your life.

Keep the dream alive,
Walk the road you must choose,
With your faith as your guide
Run the race, win or lose.

When the journey is true,
God will bless it for you.
It's your dream, it's your cause,
It's your life.

Challenges come,
Tears multiply,
But with love on your side
You'll continue to try.

Keep the dream alive,
Overcome any fear.
Standing strong, face the wrong,
Never quit, persevere.

When the journey is true,
Then it's all up to you
To pursue, carry on,
It's your life.

Some say, "You can't,"
Others, "You could."
You'll achieve what you must
'Cause you know that you should.

Keep the dream alive
In your heart, in your soul,
Don't give up on the prize,
Keep your eyes on the goal.

When the journey is true,
God will bless it for you.
It's your dream, it's your cause,
It's your life.

Keep the Dream Alive

Words and Music by Glen Aubrey

(1.) Chal - - - len - ges come, tears mul - ti -
(2.) Some say, "You can't," oth - - - ers, "You
ply, but with love on your side you'll con -
could." You'll a - chieve what you must 'cause you
tin - ue to try. Keep the dream a -
know that you should. Keep the dream a -
live, o - ver - come an - y fear. Stand - ing strong, face the
live, in your heart, in your soul, don't give up on the
wrong, nev - er quit, per - se - vere. When the
prize, keep your eyes on the goal. When the
jour - - - ney is true, then it's all up to
jour - - - ney is true, God will bless it for
you to pur - sue, car - ry on, it's your
you. It's your dream, it's your cause, it's your
life. life.

Chapter 8
Sovereignty

...that this nation, under God, shall have a new birth of freedom—

The times come when people would simply like to start over, erase the sins of the past, correct gross errors in judgment, and rid their environments of pervasive injustices. They want a new birth. Starting over reconstitutes the future, reestablishes enduring principles, and captures the perspectives of fresh ideas.

Exemplary leaders view new-start opportunities with both humility and determination. It takes a humble person to realize that changes must occur within a broken system, especially one they have led. It takes a determined leader to initiate and complete the necessary improvements.

Great leaders comprehend that what they don't know exceeds what they do know. These leaders are humble enough to learn and determined enough to educate, act, and design destinies.

Leadership submits when it recognizes that needs for improvements exist. Leadership perseveres when it determines a course of action is right.

Effective leaders understand that service *to* their people comes before requiring service *from* their people. When the needs for new births are revealed these leaders willfully submit to worthwhile causes on behalf of their followers and themselves. They know that humility is never a demonstration of weakness and that fixed determination must follow correct decisions. Leaders best serve those who follow by initially demonstrating humility and determination, paving the paths on which others will walk.

If you are the leader, to what or whom are you in willful submission? If the answer to that question is no one, your leadership is guaranteed to not be effective in the long run, although you may make waves today and even win elections.

Ego displayed in dignity and confidence is healthy. It rightfully submits when it should. It exercises self-controlled strength. On the contrary, egotism showcased in arrogance is faulty at its core. It demonstrates vast insecurity as it bullies its way through.

Everyone is in submission to someone or some entity. Desires for new births position great leaders to humble themselves before higher authority and fulfill notable causes with determination. Confidence born of both blessings from the outside and assurance on the inside demonstrates a leader's balance and maturity.

Lincoln was submissive to God. There is absolutely no doubt of this fact. Read the Gettysburg Address. Then read Lincoln's Second Inaugural Address. Then read them both again.

It is said that Lincoln added the phrase *"under God"* while sitting on the platform just before delivering the speech. Whether true or not that he added the phrase at that time, the phrase has become part of this oration ever since it was delivered.

These two words, *"under God,"* reveal some of this president's world view and belief system. An important point is this: Exemplary leadership chooses humility before God and dedication to a purpose proven to be of higher importance than self absorption or exaggerated promotion.

This president admitted he did not understand God's designs fully. Who does? However, Lincoln knew he was part of them.

There are many examples. During September of 1862 Lincoln wrote his "Meditation on the Divine Will." *"The will of God prevails. In great contests each party claims to act in accordance with the will of God. Both may be, and one must be, wrong."*

In a letter to Albert Hodges dated April 4, 1864, Lincoln stated, *"If God now wills the removal of a great wrong, and wills also that we of the North as well as you of the South, shall pay fairly for our complicity in that wrong, impartial history will find therein new cause to attest and revere the justice and goodness of God."*

Later that same year, in a letter dated September 4 and addressed to Eliza Gurney, he wrote, *"We hoped for a happy termination of this terrible war long before this; but God knows best, and has ruled otherwise. We shall yet acknowledge His wisdom and our own error therein."*

March 4, 1865 was the date on which Lincoln gave his immortal Second Inaugural Address. Note particularly the references to God, His sovereignty, judgment, and righteousness in this excerpt.

> *"Both read the same Bible, and pray to the same God; and each invokes His aid against the other. It may seem strange that any men should dare to ask a just God's assistance in wringing their bread from the sweat of other men's faces; but let us judge not that we be not judged. The prayers of both could*

not be answered; that of neither has been answered fully. The Almighty has His own purposes. 'Woe unto the world because of offenses; for it must needs be that offenses come, but woe to that man by whom the offense cometh.' If we shall suppose that American slavery is one of those offenses which, in the providence of God, must needs come, but which, having continued through His appointed time, He now wills to remove, and that He gives to both North and South this terrible war as the woe due to those by whom the offense came, shall we discern therein any departure from those divine attributes which the believers in a living God always ascribe to Him? Fondly do we hope, fervently do we pray, that this mighty scourge of war may speedily pass away. Yet, if God wills that it continue until all the wealth piled by the bondsman's two hundred and fifty years of unrequited toil shall be sunk, and until every drop of blood drawn with the lash shall be paid by another drawn with the sword, as was said three thousand years ago, so still it must be said 'the judgments of the Lord are true and righteous altogether.'"

Consider: To whom or what do you willingly submit? For what cause is your determination declared and demonstrated?

The phrase *new birth of freedom* is profound. Lincoln knew that the nation was in peril at the time of this speech. He humbled himself before God as he earnestly hoped, strongly desired, and worked diligently for this country to survive.

People remembered that the United States had birthed its own freedom in 1776. In 1863 they began to realize it was up to them to re-create their country all over again. This time, however, the country would prevent separation and severance, not position them. This time the forces to uphold the nation would declare that the Union was perpetual, that no part of it could willfully depart, regardless of the reasons.

A new birth of freedom would be composed of multiple layers, stretch over lengthy timelines, and would not be devoid of intense struggle. The country's history would prove that many additional new births and accompanying freedoms would become parts of its heritage, each with their own degrees of sacrifice.

Release from bondage for those held as slaves would constitute one example of a new birth. Removing the shackles that had framed the long-festering divisions and acts of secession had been a core desire of Lincoln.

Even though the Emancipation Proclamation had been signed and was already eleven months old, the end to slavery would not come during Lincoln's life. The 13th Amendment to the Constitution of the United States would be adopted eight months after his death.

It was ratified on December 6, 1865.

Its words are simple and strong. Section 1: "Neither slavery nor involuntary servitude, except as punishment for crime whereof the party shall have been duly convicted, shall exist within the United States, or any place subject to their jurisdiction." Section 2: "Congress shall have power to enforce this article by appropriate legislation."

The passage of the Civil Rights Act in 1964 composed another new birth of freedom emerging from the eradication of slavery. Racism continued after the Civil War; it remained throughout the 20th Century in spite of the law. In this new century its ugly face still emerges, but it is dying—because it must.

Lincoln had signed the Emancipation Proclamation on January 1, 1863. Today we know this document did far more than free the slaves to fight for the Union although this facet was indeed part of its purpose. The bottom line was this: Lincoln wanted all people everywhere to be free.

The story is told that just before he put his signature to the document he noted he had been shaking hands with several hundred people at a White House event. His hand was trembling because of all of this activity. Lincoln expressed concern that if his signature wavered, it might show a lack of commitment to what he was doing. But with determination, convinced his action was right, he signed the proclamation. It's a strong signature.

As a leader, your signature—a symbol of the roles and responsibilities that you embrace—represents your unwavering dedication to decisions you know to be right. When you or any leader are so committed, actions based on abiding truths will not be unnecessarily swayed by diverse opinions of opponents or mounting adverse circumstances.

Freedom is never free. Preserving it includes acts of immense sacrifice. New births of freedom guarantee the longevity of a system of government, demonstrated to be the best the world had ever seen.

Assurance of a positive outcome will always be based on truth. Confidence exists when a leader's decision-making and action rest on immovable principle.

Here's the point: When a wise leader recognizes the need for a new birth of freedom that leader chooses humility. When positive changes are desired that leader submits to higher authority. He or she makes choices based on abiding principles. The leader acts on those principles with determination. Results outlast persons, circumstances, and the opinions of any era.

Chapter 9
Government

...and that government of the people, by the people, for the people...

In three small phrases, Lincoln summarized the essence of representative government. A government is representative when it is:

1. *Of the people:* The people create it—it emerges from them and they uphold it.
2. *By the people:* The people mold it—it works through them.
3. *For the people:* The people benefit from it—it works on their behalf.

Make no mistake: Those who are elected represent their constituencies best when they serve the people who placed them in office. The government of a free people exists to benefit those it governs. In this form of rule those who are governed do not exist to serve their government.

Despotism reigns when a government denies the freedoms its people were guaranteed in their constitution. Rights can be eroded over time. Every generation must be vigilant to protect and exercise the liberties designed and declared in their founding documents. Beware of any government or administration that seeks to restrict or redefine the freedoms of its citizenry in violation of the people's shared and agreed values.

Lincoln honored the people and their liberties by upholding the Declaration of Independence and the Constitution of the United States. In his concluding phrases of the Gettysburg Address he placed enduring and resonating themes from those original documents into common understanding and application.

Of the people spoke of origin, purpose, and perpetuity. The Declaration of Independence represented the birth of a new nation, and more. The document declared that the nation was to be founded upon, and dedicated to, preserving a citizen's inherent rights. Here is the actual text: "We hold these truths to be self-evident, that all men are created equal, that they are endowed by their Creator with certain unalienable Rights, that among these are Life, Liberty and the pursuit of Happiness."

Wars are fought over beliefs. Lincoln's conviction, shared by the majority of Americans in the North, was that a Union founded on the propositions of its original documents was worth saving, even through war. Remember, the conflict-ridden nation had endured immense losses by the time of the Gettysburg conflict. It would suffer many more following the battle and the address.

Because the United States was a nation *of* the people the president articulated the ultimate hope that the will of its people, to save and preserve their country, would prevail. He understood this dedication included sacrifice. Leaders recognize and endorse this truth: A principle embraced must be followed by the duty required to uphold it.

By the people meant that the citizens of the country could mold their nation's character. In lawful elections, the will of the majority becomes known. A country's character is fashioned when laws are passed that reflect the desires of the electorate.

Lincoln correctly understood that good people may possess strong and opposing opinions regarding any issue. Destroying the Union, however, was not an issue worthy of consideration on any front.

Lincoln never referred to the Confederacy as a separate

country. He considered the Confederacy to be composed of states in rebellion against the United States (see the text of the Emancipation Proclamation on page 143).

On February 3, 1865, peace talks at Hampton Roads, Virginia failed because the participation from the North required reuniting the nation and the emancipation of slaves, two conditions the South would not accept. The South entered the talks with the stipulation of acceptance of independence, a premise which Lincoln refused.

Secession would not be permitted. Severance was not possible. Permanent separation would never be allowed. Rebellion would be done away with. Lincoln unreservedly had declared his commitment to restore the Union.

In his First Inaugural Address delivered on March 4, 1861, the President stated unequivocally:

"In your hands, my dissatisfied fellow-countrymen, and not in mine, is the momentous issue of civil war. The Government will not assail you. You can have no conflict without being yourselves the aggressors. You have no oath registered in heaven to destroy the Government, while I shall have the most solemn one to 'preserve, protect, and defend it.'"

Citizens mold the nation's character under their constitution. This is the responsibility exercised *by the people*.

The phrase *for the people* may have been received by Lincoln's audience on several levels, all related, none contradictory. One was historical. The nation had come into being on behalf of those who had desired it for themselves and their posterity. The Civil War was being fought to restore the national authority for the people. The nation would be stronger as one country, not two. Therefore, the government would not allow any group to dictate otherwise.

Another meaning of the word *for* was contemporary. Lincoln understood that the Civil War could never be divorced from slavery, perhaps one of the country's greatest trials and scourges, and that slavery had contributed to the cause of the rebellion. He wanted an end to its presence and a restored and unified nation on behalf of all of its people.

In his Second Inaugural, on March 6, 1865, Lincoln declared:

"Both parties deprecated war, but one of them would make war rather than let the nation survive, and the other would accept war rather than let it perish, and the war came. One-eighth of the whole population were colored slaves, not distributed generally over the Union, but localized in the southern part of it. These slaves constituted a peculiar and powerful interest. All knew that this interest was somehow the cause of the war. To strengthen, perpetuate, and extend this interest was the object for which the insurgents would rend the

Union even by war, while the Government claimed no right to do more than to restrict the territorial enlargement of it."

A third view of *for* was futuristic. Lincoln possessed a broad and holistic outlook on behalf of Americans yet unborn. He understood that a government that worked for its people in perpetuity would have to endure many tests, even ones as severe as slavery and severance. Lincoln's desire was expressed for those of every age who would call themselves American. He wanted the country to remain united and its citizens to be free for all time.

The lesson here is this: A leader firmly remains not dissuaded from right causes no matter the degrees of difficulty. When the decision to uphold a true principle is declared, a great leader shall not be deterred.

Dedicated leaders honor and uphold the highest goals for the greatest good. Preserving a government *of the people, by the people, for the people* certainly represents one of those goals. A nation so committed provisions and protects what it treasures most: the rights and freedoms of its citizens.

Chapter 10
Endurance

...shall not perish from the earth.

What really can be considered *permanent*? What truly can be designed to last for all time?

Look around you on a clear night. The earth and stars display unimaginable degrees of endurance. We are told that over 100 billion galaxies exist in addition to our own. Science informs us that the universe continues to expand. To our finite understanding it is limitless. Who can comprehend such an awesome and abiding creation?

What endures for you? What shapes your perspectives and beliefs? What lasts beyond you? On what can you really rely besides death, taxes, and the fact that tomorrow is coming whether or not you are prepared for it?

When he chose the phrase *shall not perish from the earth* to conclude the Gettysburg Address Lincoln knew that indeed there remained a distinct possibility that the country he had known could cease to exist unless the national authority was restored. Recall that at the time of the oration the future of the nation was in no way decided or secure.

And here's the point: Leaders who understand their purpose, place, and responsibility recognize that consequences are not optional. Results always follow actions, good or bad. These leaders prepare for consequences as well as try to fashion them.

Knowledgeable leaders accept this principle: Effects endure beyond the events that give them life. Those in charge learn the beneficial truths each era teaches. They strive to produce uplifting outcomes and prevent negative results. They recall history's lessons, knowing these shape the minds and means of generations—theirs and those that are to come.

Lincoln could not foresee the threats that were to unfold and shape this country. He could not predict the concerns or conflicts that would involve the United States in the 20th and 21st centuries: World War I (1914 – 1918), World War II (1939 – 1945), the Korean War (1950 – 1953), the rise of Fidel Castro in Cuba (beginning 1959) and the Bay of Pigs (1961), the Cold

War (1945 – 1991) and the Berlin Wall (1961 – 1989), Vietnam (US involvement 1961 – 1973), Grenada (1983), Saddam Hussein's invasion of Kuwait and Operation Desert Storm (1990 – 1991), the terrorist attacks on the World Trade Center (1993) and on the *USS Cole* (2000), and the tragic events of September 11, 2001 resulting in Operation Enduring Freedom and the Global War on Terror (beginning 2001), and the War for Iraqi Freedom (beginning 2003).

What Lincoln could see, however, was that no matter the severity of the battles, where the conflicts were to be located, or who the enemy was the United States would remain a guarantor and grantor of freedom. According to Lincoln, this nation should not perish from the earth or shirk from the duties its presence demanded.

Preserving the country was an eternal cause. It originated in the rights and responsibilities of a free people who would govern themselves. This arrangement was for all time. It was destined to endure for its citizens and impact its world forever.

This is permanence. The survival and endurance of the United States would produce an abiding faith in this maxim: What one generation gives in sacrifice, future generations receive in liberty.

Could the country perish in the Civil War? Could this nation destroy itself?

Freedom is not guaranteed unless a free people are watchful, willing to pay the necessary price to assure longevity. Perpetuity of a free republic is never an iron clad pledge harbored in isolation, removed from threats and conflicts.

Freedom faces onslaughts. It has to. Freedom-loving people know vigilance is required if a nation *"so conceived and so dedicated"* is to endure. A country committed to permanent survival has to be bold, engaged, and staunch in its resolve. It must fight for what it believes its destiny to be whenever that destiny is threatened.

Assaults to liberty will not cease. The original and founding principles of the United States may be reinterpreted, ripped and shredded, discarded from within and dismissed from without by those who do not cherish what this country stands for.

People who enjoy the rights declared in the Declaration of Independence, the Constitution, and Bill of Rights will defend these rights because they value them. Devoted individuals are those "...Who more than self their country loved, And mercy more than life."*

Freedom-loving men and women do whatever it takes to assure freedom for themselves and those who follow. Each generation of Americans is presented with the unique opportunity and sacred privilege to honor the Constitution of the United States. Every four years the President of the United States takes this oath of office:

> "I do solemnly swear (or affirm) that I will faithfully execute the Office of President of the United States, and will to the best of my Ability, preserve, protect and defend the Constitution of the United States."

Assuming and performing the duties of the highest office of this land are tasks not easily done, nor should they be. Risks abound. Our government is run by its people and people are fallible. Mistakes will be made. Whoever the president is, and whoever makes up the Congress of the United States and the Supreme Court, they are all individuals with limited understanding and restricted powers of judgment.

The perpetual union of the United States is guaranteed first by the *desire* of an informed, though imperfect, populace. These people want their country to remain free and strive to preserve that freedom.

These people elect representatives to the Congress and a leader to the Office of the President who affirm their beliefs. "We the People" *trust* our leaders to fulfill their responsibilities with integrity.

Desire and *trust* are two immovable and foundational characteristics of those who cherish liberty. When desire and trust are shared by the people and their representatives, this cooperation provides the highest motivation for the United

States to remain a strong and sovereign nation.

Remember that Lincoln's obligation was to uphold the Constitution and restore the national unity—he had stated this. The people desired and trusted his leadership. They elected him twice.

As man of integrity who practiced law he once said, *"Discourage litigation. Persuade your neighbors to compromise whenever you can. As a peacemaker the lawyer has superior opportunity of being a good man. There will still be business enough."*

As a savvy politician, Lincoln understood campaigning and building alliances. His political career was marked with both.

As an elected official, he committed himself to the cause he swore an oath to uphold: to honor the desires of those who had entrusted him with lofty responsibility. He considered himself to be a servant of the people and their Constitution.

A resounding truth is this: Great leaders stand for the right and serve well the people who elect them when they lead them with integrity, honoring the people's desire and trust. Leadership fulfills its duties and inspires followers to complete theirs in a society that cherishes liberty.

The concluding words of the Gettysburg Address offer hope to committed leaders and followers who perform the obligations of preserving freedom:

- "We the People" assure this country's permanence by participating fully in the process of representative government. People who care get involved.
- "We the People" must elect those who best represent the views of the electorate they are sworn to serve. If those we choose fail or commit fault, in the proper time and method we will replace them with others who will honor our desires and fulfill our trust.
- When "We the People" speak, office holders should listen. If they don't, their tasks will be given to others who will.
- When "We the People" desire change we will fully engage in lawful processes to assure that our government serves us.
- Here's the principle: It is we who provide the guarantee of perpetuity.

People so committed are those who believe that these United States "*…under God, shall have a new birth of freedom—and that government of the people, by the people, for the people, shall not perish from the earth.*"

Conclusions are evidenced in actions. Decisions live in duty. Let us not shrink from the responsibilities we possess. Let us embrace them, fulfill them, and finish well.

Let us learn from Lincoln and emulate his leadership model. When we do, we will benefit the people of today and assure liberty for those of tomorrow. Our contributions will become defining moments of greatness for us and our posterity.

* *Lyrics to "America the Beautiful"*

Epilogue

"Let us have faith that right makes might, and in that faith, let us, to the end, dare to do our duty as we understand it."

These are the closing words of Lincoln's Cooper Union Address, delivered at New York, New York, on February 27, 1860. Following the event a New York writer penned, "No man ever before made such an impression on his first appeal to a New York audience." We might add that no man in American history has retained more enduring appeal since. Lincoln's words touched the nation and the world, and continue to do so.

For people who desire to embrace a lasting and positive leadership model there are few models, if any, that compare to the one provided by Lincoln. The principles espoused in the Gettysburg Address and evidenced in the life of our sixteenth president provide standards to which developing leaders should aspire.

Students of Lincoln discover defining moments of greatness in his words and deeds. These individuals are inspired to perform their duties and finish well. Their contributions provide examples to those whose turns are next.

In the final analysis: Patriots are students of history actively engaged in the present, who protect and defend the principles of freedom upon which the country was founded. They embrace responsibility and build on behalf of future generations. They sacrifice to ensure liberty. These citizens are the guarantors of the rights we hold dear. These people assure that the United States of America remains a strong and sovereign land.

First Inaugural Address
Abraham Lincoln
March 4, 1861

Fellow-Citizens of the United States:

In compliance with a custom as old as the Government itself, I appear before you to address you briefly and to take in your presence the oath prescribed by the Constitution of the United States to be taken by the President "before he enters on the execution of this office."

I do not consider it necessary at present for me to discuss those matters of administration about which there is no special anxiety or excitement.

Apprehension seems to exist among the people of the southern States that by the accession of a Republican Administration their property and their peace and personal security are to be endangered. There has never been any reasonable cause for such apprehension.

Indeed, the most ample evidence to the contrary has all the while existed and been open to their inspection. It is found in nearly all the published speeches of him who now addresses you. I do but quote from one of those speeches when I declare that—

I have no purpose, directly or indirectly, to interfere with the institution of slavery in the States where it exists. I believe I have no lawful right to do so, and I have no inclination to do so.

Those who nominated and elected me did so with full knowledge that I had made this and many similar declarations and had never recanted them; and more than this, they placed in the platform for my acceptance, and as a law to themselves and to me, the clear and emphatic resolution which I now read:

Resolved, That the maintenance inviolate of the rights of the States, and especially the right of each State to order and control its own domestic institutions according to its own judgment exclusively, is essential to that balance of power on which the perfection and endurance of our political fabric depend; and we denounce the lawless invasion by armed force of the soil of any State or Territory, no matter what pretext, as among the gravest of crimes.

I now reiterate these sentiments, and in doing so I only press upon the public attention the most conclusive evidence of which the case is susceptible that the property, peace, and security of no section are to be in any wise endangered by the now incoming Administration. I add, too, that all the protection which, consistently with the Constitution and the laws, can be given will be cheerfully given to all the States when lawfully demanded, for whatever cause—as cheerfully to one section as to another.

There is much controversy about the delivering up of fugitives from service or labor. The clause I now read is as plainly written in the Constitution as any other of its provisions:

No person held to service or labor in one State, under the laws thereof, escaping into another, shall in consequence of any law or regulation therein be discharged from such service or labor, but shall be delivered up on claim of the party to whom such service or labor may be due.

It is scarcely questioned that this provision was intended by those who made it for the reclaiming of what we call fugitive slaves; and the intention of the lawgiver is the law. All members of Congress swear their support to the whole Constitution—to this provision as much as to any other. To the proposition, then, that slaves whose cases come within the terms of this clause "shall be delivered up" their oaths are unanimous. Now, if they would make the effort in good temper, could they not with nearly equal unanimity frame and pass a law by means of which to keep good that unanimous oath?

There is some difference of opinion whether this clause should be enforced by national or by State authority, but surely that difference is not a very material one. If the slave is to be surrendered, it can be of but little consequence to him or to others by which authority it is done. And should anyone in any case be content that his oath shall go unkept on a merely unsubstantial controversy as to how it shall be kept?

Again: In any law upon this subject ought not

all the safeguards of liberty known in civilized and humane jurisprudence to be introduced, so that a free man be not in any case surrendered as a slave? And might it not be well at the same time to provide by law for the enforcement of that clause in the Constitution which guarantees that "the citizens of each State shall be entitled to all privileges and immunities of citizens in the several States"?

I take the official oath to-day with no mental reservations and with no purpose to construe the Constitution or laws by any hypercritical rules; and while I do not choose now to specify particular acts of Congress as proper to be enforced, I do suggest that it will be much safer for all, both in official and private stations, to conform to and abide by all those acts which stand unrepealed than to violate any of them trusting to find impunity in having them held to be unconstitutional.

It is seventy-two years since the first inauguration of a President under our National Constitution. During that period fifteen different and greatly distinguished citizens have in succession administered the executive branch of the Government. They have conducted it through many perils, and generally with great success. Yet, with all this scope of precedent, I now enter upon the same task for the brief constitutional term of four years under great and peculiar difficulty. A disruption of the Federal Union, heretofore only menaced, is now formidably attempted.

I hold that in contemplation of universal law and of the Constitution the Union of these States is perpetual. Perpetuity is implied, if not expressed, in the fundamental law of all national governments. It is safe to assert that no government proper ever had a provision in its organic law for its own termination. Continue to execute all the express provisions of our National Constitution, and the Union will endure forever, it being impossible to destroy it except by some action not provided for in the instrument itself.

Again: If the United States be not a government proper, but an association of States in the nature of contract merely, can it, as a contract, be peaceably unmade by less than all the parties who made it? One party to a contract may violate it—break it, so to speak—but does it not require all to lawfully rescind it?

Descending from these general principles, we find the proposition that in legal contemplation the Union is perpetual confirmed by the history of the Union itself. The Union is much older than the Constitution. It was formed, in fact, by the Articles of Association in 1774. It was matured and continued by the Declaration of Independence in 1776. It was further matured, and the faith of all the then thirteen States expressly plighted and engaged that it should be perpetual, by the Articles of Confederation in 1778. And finally, in 1787, one of the declared objects for ordaining and establishing the Constitution was "to form a more perfect Union."

But if destruction of the Union by one or by a part only of the States be lawfully possible, the Union is less perfect than before the Constitution, having lost the vital element of perpetuity.

It follows from these views that no State upon its own mere motion can lawfully get out of the Union; that resolves and ordinances to that effect are legally void, and that acts of violence within any State or States against the authority of the United States are insurrectionary or revolutionary, according to circumstances.

I therefore consider that in view of the Constitution and the laws the Union is unbroken, and to the extent of my ability, I shall take care, as the Constitution itself expressly enjoins upon me, that the laws of the Union be faithfully executed in all the States. Doing this I deem to be only a simple duty on my part, and I shall perform it so far as practicable unless my rightful masters, the American people, shall withhold the requisite means or in some authoritative manner direct the contrary. I trust this will not be regarded as a menace, but only as the declared purpose of the Union that it will constitutionally defend and maintain itself.

In doing this there needs to be no bloodshed or violence, and there shall be none unless it be forced upon the national authority. The power confided to me will be used to hold, occupy, and possess the property and places belonging to the Government and to collect the duties and imposts; but beyond what may be necessary for these objects, there will be no invasion, no using of force against or among the people anywhere. Where hostility to the United States in any interior locality shall be so great and universal as to prevent competent resident citizens from holding the Federal offices, there will be no attempt to force obnoxious strangers among the people for that object. While the strict legal right may exist in the Government to enforce the exercise of these offices, the attempt to do so would be so irritating and so nearly impracticable withal that I deem it better to forego for the time the uses of such offices.

The mails, unless repelled, will continue to be furnished in all parts of the Union. So far as possible the people everywhere shall have that sense of perfect security which is most favorable to calm thought and reflection. The course here indicated will be followed unless current events and experience shall show a modification or change to be proper, and in every case and exigency my best discretion will be exercised, according to circumstances actually existing and with a view and a hope of a peaceful solution of the national troubles and the restoration of fraternal sympathies and affections.

That there are persons in one section or another who seek to destroy the Union at all events and are glad of any pretext to do it I will neither affirm nor deny; but if there be such, I need address no word to them. To those, however, who really love the Union may I not speak?

Before entering upon so grave a matter as the destruction of our national fabric, with all its benefits, its memories, and its hopes, would it not be wise to ascertain precisely why we do it? Will you hazard so desperate a step while there is any possibility that any portion of the ills you fly from have no real existence? Will you, while the certain ills you fly to are greater than all the real ones you fly from, will you risk the commission of so fearful a mistake?

All profess to be content in the Union if all constitutional rights can be maintained. Is it true, then, that any right plainly written in the Constitution has been denied? I think not. Happily, the human mind is so constituted that no party can reach to the audacity of doing this. Think, if you can, of a single instance in which a plainly written provision of the Constitution has ever been denied. If by the mere force of numbers a majority should deprive a minority of any clearly written constitutional right, it might in a moral point of view justify revolution; certainly would if such right were a vital one. But such is not our case. All the vital rights of minorities and of individuals are so plainly assured to them by affirmations and negations, guaranties and prohibitions, in the Constitution that controversies never arise concerning them. But no organic law can ever be framed with a provision specifically applicable to every question which may occur in practical administration. No foresight can anticipate nor any document of reasonable length contain express provisions for all possible questions. Shall fugitives from labor be surrendered by national or by State authority? The Constitution does not expressly say. May Congress prohibit slavery in the Territories? The Constitution does not expressly say. Must Congress protect slavery in the Territories? The

Constitution does not expressly say.

From questions of this class spring all our constitutional controversies, and we divide upon them into majorities and minorities. If the minority will not acquiesce, the majority must, or the Government must cease. There is no other alternative, for continuing the Government is acquiescence on one side or the other. If a minority in such case will secede rather than acquiesce, they make a precedent which in turn will divide and ruin them, for a minority of their own will secede from them whenever a majority refuses to be controlled by such minority. For instance, why may not any portion of a new confederacy a year or two hence arbitrarily secede again, precisely as portions of the present Union now claim to secede from it? All who cherish disunion sentiments are now being educated to the exact temper of doing this.

Is there such perfect identity of interests among the States to compose a new union as to produce harmony only and prevent renewed secession?

Plainly the central idea of secession is the

essence of anarchy. A majority held in restraint by constitutional checks and limitations, and always changing easily with deliberate changes of popular opinions and sentiments, is the only true sovereign of a free people. Whoever rejects it does of necessity fly to anarchy or to despotism. Unanimity is impossible. The rule of a minority, as a permanent arrangement, is wholly inadmissible; so that, rejecting the majority principle, anarchy or despotism in some form is all that is left.

I do not forget the position assumed by some that constitutional questions are to be decided by the Supreme Court, nor do I deny that such decisions must be binding in any case upon the parties to a suit as to the object of that suit, while they are also entitled to very high respect and consideration in all parallel cases by all other departments of the Government. And while it is obviously possible that such decision may be erroneous in any given case, still the evil effect following it, being limited to that particular case, with the chance that it may be overruled and never become a precedent for other cases, can better be borne than could the evils of a different practice. At the same time, the candid citizen must confess that if the policy of the Government upon vital questions affecting the whole people is to be irrevocably fixed by decisions of the Supreme Court, the instant they are made in ordinary litigation between parties in personal actions the people will have ceased to be their own rulers, having to that extent practically resigned their Government into the hands of that eminent tribunal. Nor is there in this view any assault upon the court or the judges. It is a duty from which they may not shrink to decide cases properly brought before them, and it is no fault of theirs if others seek to turn their decisions to political purposes.

One section of our country believes slavery is right and ought to be extended, while the other believes it is wrong and ought not to be extended. This is the only substantial dispute. The fugitive-slave clause of the Constitution and the law for the suppression of the foreign slave trade are each as well enforced, perhaps, as any law can ever be in a community where the moral sense of the people imperfectly supports the law itself. The great body of the people abide by the dry legal obligation in both cases, and a few break over in each. This, I think, can not be perfectly cured, and it would be worse in both cases after the separation of the sections than before. The foreign slave trade, now imperfectly suppressed, would be ultimately revived without restriction in one section, while fugitive slaves, now only partially surrendered, would not be surrendered at all by the other.

Physically speaking, we can not separate. We can not remove our respective sections from each other nor build an impassable wall between them. A husband and wife may be divorced and go out of the presence and beyond the reach of each other, but the different parts of our country can not do this. They can not but remain face to face, and intercourse, either amicable or hostile, must continue between them. Is it possible, then, to make that intercourse more advantageous or more satisfactory after separation than before? Can aliens make treaties easier than friends can make laws? Can treaties be more faithfully enforced between aliens than laws can among friends? Suppose you go to war, you can not fight always; and when, after much loss on both sides and no gain on either, you cease fighting, the identical old questions, as to terms of intercourse, are again upon you.

This country, with its institutions, belongs to the people who inhabit it. Whenever they shall grow weary of the existing Government, they can exercise their constitutional right of amending it or their revolutionary right to dismember or overthrow it. I can not be ignorant of the fact that many worthy and patriotic citizens are desirous of having the National Constitution amended. While I make no recommendation of amendments, I fully recognize the rightful authority of the people over the whole subject, to be exercised in either of the modes prescribed in the instrument itself; and I should, under existing circumstances, favor rather than oppose a fair opportunity being afforded the people to act upon it. I will venture to add that to me the convention mode seems preferable, in that it allows amendments to originate with the people themselves, instead of only permitting them to take or reject propositions originated by others, not especially chosen for the purpose, and which might not be precisely such as they would wish to either accept or refuse. I understand a proposed amendment to the Constitution—which amendment, however, I have not seen—has passed Congress, to the effect that the Federal Government shall never interfere with the domestic institutions of the States, including that of persons held to service. To avoid misconstruction of what I have said, I depart from my purpose not to speak of particular amendments so far as to say that, holding such a provision to now be implied constitutional law, I have no objection to its being made express and irrevocable.

The Chief Magistrate derives all his authority from the people, and they have referred none upon him to fix terms for the separation of the States. The people themselves can do this if also they choose, but the Executive as such has nothing to do with it. His duty is to administer the present Government as it came to his hands and to transmit it unimpaired by him to his successor.

Why should there not be a patient confidence in the ultimate justice of the people? Is there any better or equal hope in the world? In our present differences, is either party without faith of being in the right? If the Almighty Ruler of Nations, with His eternal truth and justice, be on your side of the North, or on yours of the South, that truth and that justice will surely prevail by the judgment of this great tribunal of the American people.

By the frame of the Government under which we live this same people have wisely given their public servants but little power for mischief, and have with equal wisdom provided for the return of that little to their own hands at very short intervals. While the people retain their virtue and vigilance no Administration by any extreme of wickedness or folly can very seriously injure the Government in the short space of four years.

My countrymen, one and all, think calmly and well upon this whole subject. Nothing valuable can be lost by taking time. If there be an object to hurry any of you in hot haste to a step which you would never take deliberately, that object will be frustrated by taking time; but no good object can be frustrated by it. Such of you as are now dissatisfied still have the old

Constitution unimpaired, and, on the sensitive point, the laws of your own framing under it; while the new Administration will have no immediate power, if it would, to change either. If it were admitted that you who are dissatisfied hold the right side in the dispute, there still is no single good reason for precipitate action. Intelligence, patriotism, Christianity, and a firm reliance on Him who has never yet forsaken this favored land are still competent to adjust in the best way all our present difficulty.

In your hands, my dissatisfied fellow-countrymen, and not in mine, is the momentous issue of civil war. The Government will not assail you. You can have no conflict without being yourselves the aggressors. You have no oath registered in heaven to destroy the Government, while I shall have the most solemn one to "preserve, protect, and defend it."

I am loath to close. We are not enemies, but friends. We must not be enemies. Though passion may have strained it must not break our bonds of affection. The mystic chords of memory, stretching from every battlefield and patriot grave to every living heart and hearthstone all over this broad land, will yet swell the chorus of the Union, when again touched, as surely they will be, by the better angels of our nature.

Second Inaugural Address
Abraham Lincoln
March 4, 1865

Fellow-Countrymen:

At this second appearing to take the oath of the Presidential office there is less occasion for an extended address than there was at the first. Then a statement somewhat in detail of a course to be pursued seemed fitting and proper. Now, at the expiration of four years, during which public declarations have been constantly called forth on every point and phase of the great contest which still absorbs the attention and engrosses the energies of the nation, little that is new could be presented. The progress of our arms, upon which all else chiefly depends, is as well known to the public as to myself, and it is, I trust, reasonably satisfactory and encouraging to all. With high hope for the future, no prediction in regard to it is ventured.

On the occasion corresponding to this four years ago all thoughts were anxiously directed to an impending civil war. All dreaded it, all sought to avert it. While the inaugural address was being delivered from this place, devoted altogether to saving the Union without war, urgent agents were in the city seeking to destroy it without war—seeking to dissolve the Union and divide effects by negotiation. Both parties deprecated war, but one of them would make war rather than let the nation survive, and the other would accept war rather than let it perish, and the war came.

One-eighth of the whole population were colored slaves, not distributed generally over the Union, but localized in the southern part of it. These slaves constituted a peculiar and powerful interest. All knew that this interest was somehow the cause of the war. To strengthen, perpetuate, and extend this interest was the object for which the insurgents would rend the Union even by war, while the Government claimed no right to do more than to restrict the territorial enlargement of it. Neither party expected for the war the magnitude or the duration which it has already attained. Neither anticipated that the cause of the conflict might cease with or even before the conflict itself should cease. Each looked for an easier triumph, and a result less fundamental and astounding. Both read the same Bible and pray to the same God, and each invokes His aid against the other. It may seem strange that any men should dare to ask a just God's assistance in wringing their bread from the sweat of other men's faces, but let us judge not, that we be not judged. The prayers of both could not be answered. That of neither has been answered fully. The Almighty has His own purposes. "Woe unto the world because of offenses; for it must needs be that offenses come, but woe to that man by whom the offense cometh." If we shall suppose that American slavery is one of those offenses which, in the providence of God, must needs come, but which, having continued through His appointed time, He now wills to remove, and that He gives to both North and South this terrible war as the woe due to those by whom the offense came, shall we discern therein any departure from those divine attributes which the believers in a living God always ascribe to Him? Fondly do we hope, fervently do we pray, that this mighty scourge of war may speedily pass away. Yet, if God wills that it continue until all the wealth piled by the bondsman's two hundred and fifty years of unrequited toil shall be sunk, and until every drop of blood drawn with the lash shall be paid by another drawn with the sword, as was said three thousand years ago, so still it must be said "the judgments of the Lord are true and righteous altogether."

With malice toward none, with charity for all, with firmness in the right as God gives us to see the right, let us strive on to finish the work we are in, to bind up the nation's wounds, to care for him who shall have borne the battle and for his widow and his orphan, to do all which may achieve and cherish a just and lasting peace among ourselves and with all nations.

The Emancipation Proclamation January 1, 1863

By the President of the United States of America: A Proclamation.

Whereas, on the twenty-second day of September, in the year of our Lord one thousand eight hundred and sixty-two, a proclamation was issued by the President of the United States, containing, among other things, the following, to wit:

"That on the first day of January, in the year of our Lord one thousand eight hundred and sixty-three, all persons held as slaves within any State or designated part of a State, the people whereof shall then be in rebellion against the United States, shall be then, thenceforward, and forever free; and the Executive Government of the United States, including the military and naval authority thereof, will recognize and

maintain the freedom of such persons, and will do no act or acts to repress such persons, or any of them, in any efforts they may make for their actual freedom.

"That the Executive will, on the first day of January aforesaid, by proclamation, designate the States and parts of States, if any, in which the people thereof, respectively, shall then be in rebellion against the United States; and the fact that any State, or the people thereof, shall on that day be, in good faith, represented in the Congress of the United States by members chosen thereto at elections wherein a majority of the qualified voters of such State shall have participated, shall, in the absence of strong countervailing testimony, be deemed conclusive evidence that such State, and the people thereof, are not then in rebellion against the United States."

Now, therefore I, Abraham Lincoln, President of the United States, by virtue of the power in me vested as Commander-in-Chief, of the Army and Navy of the United States in time of actual armed rebellion against the authority and government of the United States, and as a fit and necessary war measure for suppressing said rebellion, do, on this first day of January, in the year of our Lord one thousand eight hundred and sixty-three, and in accordance with my purpose so to do publicly proclaimed for the full period of one hundred days, from the day first above mentioned, order and designate as the States and parts of States wherein the people thereof respectively, are this day in rebellion against the United States, the following, to wit:

Arkansas, Texas, Louisiana, (except the Parishes of St. Bernard, Plaquemines, Jefferson, St. John, St. Charles, St. James Ascension, Assumption, Terrebonne, Lafourche, St. Mary, St. Martin, and Orleans, including the City of New Orleans) Mississippi, Alabama, Florida, Georgia, South Carolina, North Carolina, and Virginia, (except the forty-eight counties designated as West Virginia, and also the counties of Berkley, Accomac, Northampton, Elizabeth City, York, Princess Ann, and Norfolk, including the cities of Norfolk and Portsmouth, and which excepted parts, are for the present, left precisely as if this proclamation were not issued.

And by virtue of the power, and for the purpose aforesaid, I do order and declare that all persons held as slaves within said designated States, and parts of States, are, and henceforward shall be free; and that the Executive government of the United States, including the military and naval authorities thereof, will recognize and maintain the freedom of said persons.

And I hereby enjoin upon the people so declared to be free to abstain from all violence, unless in necessary self-defence; and I recommend to them that, in all cases when allowed, they labor faithfully for reasonable wages.

And I further declare and make known, that such persons of suitable condition, will be received into the armed service of the United States to garrison forts, positions, stations, and other places, and to man vessels of all sorts in said service.

And upon this act, sincerely believed to be an act of justice, warranted by the Constitution, upon military necessity, I invoke the considerate judgment of mankind, and the gracious favor of Almighty God.

In witness whereof, I have hereunto set my hand and caused the seal of the United States to be affixed.

Done at the City of Washington, this first day of January, in the year of our Lord one thousand eight hundred and sixty three, and of the Independence of the United States of America the eighty-seventh.

By the President: ABRAHAM LINCOLN
WILLIAM H. SEWARD, Secretary of State.

Bibliography

Kunhardt, Jr., Philip B. *A New Birth of Freedom Lincoln at Gettysburg*. Boston: Little, Brown and Company, 1983.

Kunhardt, Jr., Philip B., Philip B. Kunhardt III, and Peter W. Kunhardt. *Lincoln An Illustrated Biography*. New York: Alfred A. Knopf, 1992.

Luvaas, Jay and Nelson, Harold W., ed. *Guide to the Battle of Gettysburg*. The U.S. Army War College Guides to Civil War Battles. Lawrence, Kansas: University Press of Kansas, 1986.

Pitts, Calista. *Gettysburg Addresses*. Gettysburg, Pennsylvania: Thomas Publications, 2000.

Acknowledgements

While the writing of *Lincoln, Leadership and Gettysburg* covers three years, the study of the life, perspectives, and practices of Abraham Lincoln represents 45 years. It has been an endeavor I have thoroughly enjoyed.

Many people have participated with me in the journey of discovery and learning. I would like to acknowledge several of them who have directly impacted the writing and production of this work. Without their assistance *Lincoln, Leadership and Gettysburg* would still be a dream.

First, I recognize my mother. As of this writing she is 93 years young. She is a staunch supporter. She read the original manuscript in three days. Her pronouncement was, "It's wonderful, definitely, absolutely." Thanks, Mom.

Jordan Peck is the Acquisitions Editor of Creative Team Publishing, (www.CreativeTeamPublishing.com). A friend of our family for many years, her dedication continues to inspire me. She was the primary editor of the book and she consistently provides the necessary balance to my creative thinking and writing. Thanks, Jordan.

Jeff Goble and Randy Beck are friends and supporters of Creative Team Resources Group, Inc. (CTRG) and of me personally. Jeff has contributed to the success of CTRG since 1998. He is a confidant, analyst, and information technology professional whose humor always keeps us going. Randy has provided web support and, with his wife Hayley, the encouragement of new ideas and improved methods. Thanks, Jeff and Randy.

Mike Atkinson is a friend with whom I have shared much professional history. He offered and provided help with initial marketing and advertising efforts. He stated it well, "We have walked this path together for a long time." Yes, we have. Thanks, Mike.

Eileen Aronhalt is a friend who is thoroughly familiar with Gettysburg, the place, the battle, and the address. I met her when she was working for a local bookstore there in 2004. What a treasure she is. She is responsible for this book's introduction in the town of Gettysburg on November 19, 2009 and is the supplier of nearly a fourth of my Lincoln library. Thanks, Eileen. "Here's your cup of coffee."

My son Justin is an amazingly talented human being. He is the designer of the cover art for this book and has created graphic art for many Creative Team Publishing books and CD's. When my wife Cindy saw the cover for *Lincoln,*

Leadership and Gettysburg her comment to Justin was, "I am so proud of your creative and artistic abilities!" Heather, Justin's sister viewed the artwork and exclaimed, "Yeah, I like it! I wouldn't change anything!" They are correct. Thanks, Justin. You are my son in whom I am well pleased.

The Author

Glen Aubrey is President and CEO of Creative Team Resources Group, Inc. (CTRG), www.ctrg.com. He is a business consultant, conference speaker, leadership trainer, author, music writer and orchestrator, and poet. He has authored *Leadership Is—How to Build Your Legacy, Industrial Strength Solutions Build Successful Work Teams!, Core Teams Work Their Principles and Practices, Growing Core Teams, Core Team Impact!, Go From the Night, Arranging Notes, L.E.A.D.—Learning, Education, Action, Destiny* and its study guide *Leadership Works, Freedom Light,* and *Lincoln, Leadership and Gettysburg.*

You are invited to visit these websites:
www.ctrg.com
www.CreativeTeamPublishing.com
www.LeadershipIs.com
www.Industrial-Strength-Solutions.com
www.CoreTeamsWork.com
www.Lincoln-Leadership-Gettysburg.com
www.GoFromTheNight.com
www.Lead52.com
www.Freedom-Light.com
www.glenaubrey.com

Creative Team Resources Group, Inc. (CTRG)

Creative
Team
Resources
Group

www.ctrg.com
www.LeadershipIs.com
www.Industrial-Strength-Solutions.com
www.CoreTeamsWork.com
www.Lead52.com
www.Lincoln-Leadership-Gettysburg.com

CTRG provides quality resources for the development of teams within organizations whose desires are to grow and develop their personnel and achieve greater results in product or service provision. CTRG gives people great information that allows them to make changes in how they live and work and does this through building core teams. Our resources include personnel training, seminars, counsel, one-on-one and small group leadership investment, books, instruction manuals, and web-based tools. Our services consist of conferences, consultation, and coaching.

Our foundational principle is that people are more important than production and relationships precede and give definition to function. The value of a person's contributions comes from that person's inherent worth. The value of the person causes the contributions a person makes to achieve even greater results.

Contact CTRG at the websites above. We will demonstrate first-hand how our team building principles can work for you. Glen Aubrey, President and CEO, along with other CTRG staff are available for speaking engagements and on-site training. CTRG looks forward to serving and working with you!

Creative Team Publishing (CTP)

Creative Team Publishing (CTP) is a division of Creative Team Resources Group, Inc. (CTRG, www.ctrg.com). CTP was formed in 2007 to publish and distribute business and team development, leadership training, and poetry books, as well as literature of inspiration, insight, human achievement, and positive general interest.

The company's commitment is to make high quality literature available and engage in excellence throughout the process of publication. Customer satisfaction is a top priority. Because CTP practices due diligence in selecting which books it will publish, CTP chooses to work with customers who meet a qualified standard of literary competence and uplifting content.

CTP is a fee-for-service publisher. Products offered include the following:

Pre-Press
1. Editing
2. Proofing
3. Revision
4. Typesetting
5. Four Color Cover Design
6. ISBN
7. Print Set-up

Post-Press
1. Product supply
2. Press releases

Contact Creative Team Publishing. Please visit our company website, www.CreativeTeamPublishing.com for information. We look forward to reviewing your literary creation.

Books by Glen Aubrey

Order these books at the websites below or from
www.CreativeTeamPublishing.com

Leadership Is— How to Build Your Legacy
www.LeadershipIs.com

Industrial Strength Solutions Build Successful Work Teams!
www.Industrial-Strength-Solutions.com

Core Teams Work Their Principles and Practices
www.CoreTeamsWork.com

L.E.A.D.—Learning, Education, Action, Destiny and its study guide, ***Leadership Works***
www.Lead52.com

Lincoln, Leadership and Gettysburg
www.Lincoln-Leadership-Gettysburg.com

Go From the Night—Journeys of Thought Meditations on Life (Poetry)
www.GoFromTheNight.com

Freedom Light— Expressions of Hope and Evidence (Poetry)
www.Freedom-Light.com

Growing Core Teams

Core Team Impact!

Arranging Notes

Music Audio CD Recordings by Glen Aubrey

Order these recordings from
www.CreativeTeamPublishing.com

Beautiful, A Symphonic Experience
Music by Lindamarie Todd and
Glen Aubrey

Born Is the King
Christmas Keyboard Reflections

The Custom Album
Piano Solos by Glen Aubrey

Reflecting Hymn
The Rock Album

What Child Is This
Glen Aubrey Solo Piano

Go From the Night Meditation
Glen Aubrey Solo Piano
Pat Kelley Guitar
Narratives

Meditation
Glen Aubrey Solo Piano

Timeless
Glen Aubrey Solo Piano

LaVergne, TN USA
29 October 2009
162427LV00004B/31/P

9 780979 735882